CATCHING
CHEATS

CATCHING CHEATS

EVERYDAY FORENSICS TO UNMASK BUSINESS FRAUD

ERIK LIE

Berrett–Koehler Publishers, Inc.

Berrett-Koehler Publishers, Inc.
1333 Broadway, Suite P100
Oakland, CA 94612-1921
Tel: (510) 817-2277
Fax: (510) 817-2278
bkconnection.com

ORDERING INFORMATION

Quantity sales. Special discounts are available on quantity purchases by corporations, associations, and others. For details, please go to bkconnection.com to see our bulk discounts or contact bookorders@bkpub.com for more information.

Individual sales. Berrett-Koehler publications are available through most bookstores. They can also be ordered directly from Berrett-Koehler: Tel: (800) 929-2929; Fax: (802) 864-7626; bkconnection.com.

Orders for college textbook / course adoption use. Please contact Berrett-Koehler: Tel: (800) 929-2929; Fax: (802) 864-7626.

Distributed to the US trade and internationally by Penguin Random House Publisher Services.

The authorized representative in the EU for product safety and compliance is EU Compliance Partner, Pärnu mnt. 139b-14, 11317 Tallinn, Estonia, www.eucompliancepartner.com, +372 5368 65 02.

Berrett-Koehler and the BK logo are registered trademarks of Berrett-Koehler Publishers, Inc.

Printed in the United States of America

Berrett-Koehler books are printed on long-lasting acid-free paper. When it is available, we choose paper that has been manufactured by environmentally responsible processes. These may include using trees grown in sustainable forests, incorporating recycled paper, minimizing chlorine in bleaching, or recycling the energy produced at the paper mill.

Cataloging-in-Publication Data is on file at the Library of Congress.
Library of Congress Control Number: 2025011605
ISBN 9798890571373 (paperback) | ISBN 9798890571380 (pdf) |
ISBN 9798890571397 (epub)

First Edition

33 32 31 30 29 28 27 26 25   10 9 8 7 6 5 4 3 2 1

Book production: Happenstance Type-O-Rama
Cover design and illustrations/interior illustrations: Eloy Sánchez-Vizcaíno Mengual

To my family

Contents

Preface ix

1 An Introduction to Forensic Methods 1

2 Salami Slicing: Collusion in the Stock Market 11

3 The Midnight Maneuver: Late Trading in Mutual Funds . . . 25

4 The Mirage of Hedge Fund Performance 41

5 Financial Façades: Earnings Management and
Accounting Manipulation 57

6 Insider Trading: When Secrets Pay Dividends 81

7 Banking's Biggest Bluff: The LIBOR Manipulation 105

8 Hindsight Is 20/20: The Stock Option Backdating Saga 121

Epilogue 145

Note 149

References 161

Acknowledgments 167

Index 169

About the Author 177

Preface

If you ain't trying to cheat a little,
you ain't likely to win much.

—RICHARD PETTY, NASCAR driver

In 1997, Apple lured Steve Jobs back as CEO at a token $1 annual salary. It also provided him with a backdoor for additional compensation. On January 19, 2000, Apple announced that it had given Jobs options to purchase ten million shares at whatever the stock price was on the grant date. A board member clarified that "Steve's stock options were granted a week ago at the then-market price and will gain value only as Apple's stock price rises." Strikingly, the stock price had already increased from $87 to $107 over that week. That meant that Jobs could use his options to buy ten million shares at a hefty $20 discount each, for a total discount of $200 million!

Steve Jobs's fortuitous grant timing was not unique. For about a decade, corporate America kept a dirty secret. In early 2003, I reviewed thousands of option grants to the most powerful corporate executives in the United States. I found that over and over again, the option grants occurred precisely when the stock prices hit rock bottom, effectively lining the pockets of the already wealthy executives. Now I could no longer consider these windfalls the result of mere luck. My discovery left me appalled and buzzing with adrenaline.

One relatively benign possibility was that executives used their inside information to grant themselves options before they expected the stock to rally, perhaps because they knew that the upcoming earnings would blow away investors. Nah, that couldn't be it, because I found that the entire stock market rallied after the grants. That left me with the shocking possibility that the grant dates were set after the fact, with the benefit of hindsight, just like Biff in *Back to the Future* traveled back in time with a sports almanac to bet on past sports games.

Using various tools to analyze the data, I proved that corporate executives had, indeed, backdated their option grants, violating all kinds of corporate rules and ethical standards. I also convinced the Securities and Exchange Commission (SEC) and the *Wall Street Journal* of the decade-long systematic fraud. This led to a massive investigation, countless lawsuits in the United States and Canada, two congressional hearings, the firings of at least seventy corporate executives, and the coveted Pulitzer Prize for Public Service to the *Wall Street Journal* in 2007. My contribution was also recognized when *Time* magazine included me on its list of the one hundred most influential people in the world—pretty surreal for a finance professor.

The option backdating scandal is one of many cases in which researchers and journalists have employed *forensic economics* to uncover misconduct. The availability of data in recent decades, along with simple statistical techniques, has provided a flashlight for detecting patterns of systematic and repeated fraud. In this book, I explain these detection methods, relying on visuals over heavy math and statistics. I include many anecdotal examples both to captivate readers and to provide deeper insights into how cheating is carried out and what its consequences are.

I focus on cheating in the business world with a particular emphasis on the financial sector, my area of expertise and an industry rife with both high-profile scandals and small-time frauds. The vast amounts of money in play might just be too tempting to resist, and the sector seems to draw unethical and greedy people. As a bonus, my focus gives you an opportunity to learn about finance and business, enabling you to strike up an intelligent dinner conversation with any hedge fund manager or at least impress your friend with some insights.

Why am I writing this book? After my own discoveries and extensive reading, I believe that I am an expert. Now I want to share my fascination and to educate people—whether they are aspiring researchers, seasoned journalists, or curious truth-seekers—about the basics of forensic economics. I want to entertain with engaging stories and clever studies. I add humor with the aid of the superb illustrations by the Barcelona-based illustrator Eloy Sánchez-Vizcaíno Mengual, such as the following figure depicting fraudsters Elizabeth Holmes of Theranos and Markus Braun of Wirecard in the midst of a heist. And, most ambitiously, I want to inspire others, including fellow researchers and journalists, to join me in uncovering systematic fraud and corruption. This is the first step in identifying and addressing weaknesses in the system, and, with further investigation and a bit of luck, we might even bring some culprits to justice.

Figure 1. Elizabeth Holmes and Markus Braun in black turtlenecks.

1

An Introduction to Forensic Methods

The goal is to turn data into information,
and information into insight.

—CARLY FIORINA, former CEO of Hewlett-Packard

Just as thousands of individual pixels come together to form an image, data points combine to create patterns. In this chapter, I introduce two methods for spotting possible deceit that are used throughout the book: *benchmarking* and checking for *distribution disruptions*. We'll warm up with Flo-Jo's cheetah-like sprints, depicted in Figure 1-1, step on the gas in a polluting Volkswagen Jetta, and then be on our way to discerning data patterns.

Benchmarking

In 1988, Florence Griffith Joyner, famously known as Flo-Jo, took the world of sports by storm. Her eclectic personal style, including a one-legged body suit and long, decorated fingernails, set her apart. And during the women's 100m quarterfinal of the Olympic trials on July 16, 1988, Flo-Jo not only won but also set a new world-record time of 10.49 seconds.

Figure 1-1. Flo-Jo's cheetah-like sprint.

How fast is that? If you've ever been timed running that distance yourself, you know it's fast. However, we need some better benchmarks than those from your high-school glory years. So here we go:

- Her closest competitor in the heat clocked in at 10.88 seconds, also very fast yet a significant distance behind when you watch YouTube videos of the race.

- Weeks before the Olympic trials, Flo-Jo had run a personal best of 10.89 seconds.

- Evelyn Ashford had set the world record four years earlier at 10.76 seconds, meaning that Flo-Jo lowered it by a staggering 0.27 seconds.

In an event for which world records are typically improved by tiny increments, Flo-Jo's time was astonishing, so much so that it remains the world record in 2025! Rumors quickly started to circulate that she had used performance-enhancing drugs. Flo-Jo consistently denied these allegations, and all her drug tests came back clean.

The example shows how benchmarks can help us identify suspicious results. Of course, a problem here is the lack of data points for suspicious results. Had we observed that all members of the same running club had shown an equal and simultaneous improvement, we would be more confident that something fishy had taken place.

Another benchmarking example involves the Volkswagen (VW) emissions scandal, known as Dieselgate. Diesel engines naturally emit nitrogen oxides (NO_x), which are harmful air pollutants. To address this, regulators have set a maximum of 0.043 grams per kilometer of NO_x emissions (labeled BENCHMARK 1 in Figure 1-2). VW claimed to have developed a cost-effective NO_x trap to comply with the standards. In 2013–2014, researchers at West Virginia University tested emission rates for VW cars using a laboratory dynamometer, the standard way of conducting emissions testing. They found that both the VW Jetta and the VW Passat were well below the limit, with emissions of 0.022 and 0.016 g/km, respectively (BENCHMARK 2 in Figure 1-2). However, when they tested the same cars under real-world driving conditions, which is more cumbersome and rarely done, they discovered dramatically higher emission levels: 0.61 to 1.5 g/km for the Jetta and 0.34 to 0.81 g/km for the Passat, far exceeding the earlier benchmarks. Shocked by their initial findings, the researchers repeated the tests over and over (hence the wide range of results) to make sure they hadn't made any errors.

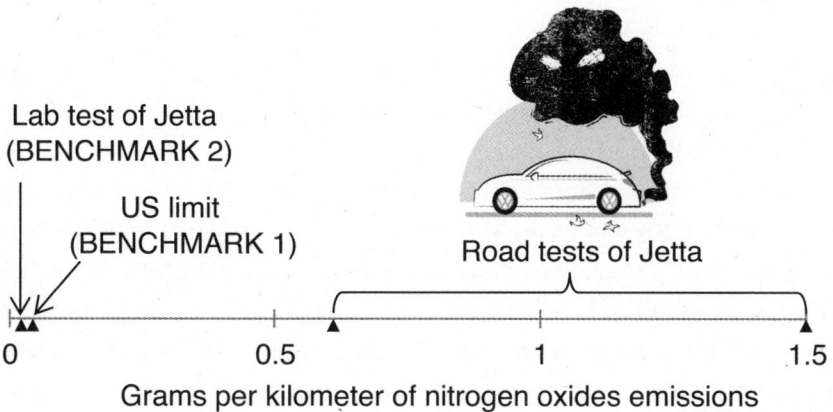

Figure 1-2. Emissions of the VW Jetta.

The scandal erupted in 2015. It turned out that VW had employed software that used speed and steering wheel movement to detect when its diesel engines were being tested, at which point the software would engage a testing mode. The testing mode turned on the NO_x trap at the cost of reduced performance and fuel economy. The scandal cost VW a whopping $100 billion in fines, customer compensation, and reputational damage.

Our first plunge into the world of finance takes us to stock analysts. These professionals value stocks and offer recommendations ranging from a strong sell (indicating the stock is overpriced) to a strong buy (indicating the stock is underpriced). However, analysts face conflicting incentives. On the one hand, they aim to provide accurate recommendations to showcase their expertise and build their reputation. On the other hand, they strive to please executives at the firms they analyze, as these executives regularly purchase investment banking services from the analysts' employers. This dynamic might produce a bullish bias, meaning that analyst recommendations lean toward buy recommendations.

In 2004, researchers Alexander Ljungqvist, Christopher Malloy, and Felicia Marston analyzed a widely used database of several hundred thousand analyst forecasts to gauge bias. If we assign values of –2 to "strong sell," –1 to "sell," 0 to "hold," +1 to "buy," and +2 to "strong buy," no bias implies an average value of 0, serving as a natural benchmark. However, the researchers found an average value of +0.6, indicating a clear bias toward buy recommendations and suggesting that the integrity of analysts was compromised.

But wait—it gets more interesting. A few years earlier, the researchers had downloaded what they believed to be the same data and found an average value of +1.2. Relative to this alternative benchmark, the bullish bias had diminished significantly, as Figure 1-3 illustrates. How could this be if the data were the same? Comparing the data sets revealed numerous additions and deletions, alterations of forecasts, and removals of analysts' names. The only reasonable explanation was that the changes were part of a systematic effort to conceal bullish bias. It seems

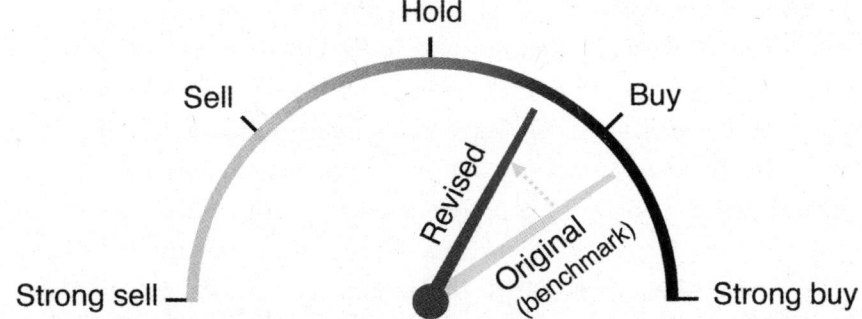

Hold

Sell

Buy

Revised

Original
(benchmark)

Strong sell

Strong buy

Figure 1-3. Original and revised analyst forecasts.

that the analysts were embarrassed by their overly optimistic forecasts intended to curry favor with their firms' clients. So, to cover up their corrupt behavior, they engaged in further fraud.

Checking for Distribution Disruptions

Most data distributions are smooth, like the distribution of heights in the population. Any disruption to the distribution, like clustering or discontinuities, warrants some reflection. For instance, if you were to inspect the distribution of heights that men report on dating apps, you would see an unusual clustering at six feet. The explanation might be innocuous: many men simply round their height to the nearest foot. A more cynical explanation is that many shorter or average-height men inflate their reported height. Plenty of anecdotal evidence supports the latter; adding a few inches to the height is supposedly common in the dating world.

Suppose instead that eight independent firms submitted identical sealed bids of $198,438.24 for a project. While underlying economic factors can lead to similar bids, there's no way that, in the absence of collusion, eight bids in the hundreds of thousands would be identical down to the penny. This is one of many examples from the Great Electrical Equipment Conspiracy, in which the largest US electrical equipment makers, including General Electric and Westinghouse, were accused of price fixing in the 1950s.

Overt illegal collusion is not just a relic of the past. For many years, the vast majority of US realtors charged exactly 6 percent for selling a property. Over time, this gradually shifted to 5 percent. In contrast, similar markets overseas typically have fees ranging from 1 percent to 3 percent. The clustering of fees at 5 percent or 6 percent in the United States, combined with the lower fees in benchmark markets, raised compelling arguments for illegal collusion. This led to a legal settlement in 2024, where the National Association of Realtors (NAR) agreed to pay over $400 million in damages and implement changes aimed at lowering fees.

Now, let's move on to some distributions that you can see for yourselves. Balázs Kovács, David Lehman, and Glenn Carroll analyzed the distribution of hygiene scores from 336,208 inspections of 27,119 restaurants conducted by 493 inspectors from 2000 to 2010 by the Los Angeles Department of Public Health. Such inspections seek to reduce incidents of foodborne illnesses and improve public health. The numerical hygiene scores are translated into letter grades like those used in the school system (with scores of 90 or above assigned a grade of A, scores in the 80s a grade of B, etc.) and displayed on a placard in the restaurant's window. An A grade is viewed as a certification of food safety and generates more visits.

Figure 1-4 shows the distribution of the hygiene scores. Impartial inspections should yield a continuous distribution, meaning a smooth distribution without jumps or pronounced clustering. That is clearly not what we see here. Rather, we see discontinuous jumps from 79 to 80 points and from 89 to 90 points, precisely the cutoffs that separate the letter grades C and B and the grades B and A, respectively. Thus, a suspiciously high number of restaurants scored well enough to secure either an A or a B, and suspiciously few ended up just below the cutoffs for an A or a B.

The analysts also discovered that the suspicious grade inflation was more prevalent for repeated interactions, meaning when an inspector had previously visited the same restaurant. Perhaps the inspectors became friendly with the restaurant owners over time and wished to help in small ways. Or perhaps good old-fashioned bribery played a role. Either way, the system is flawed.

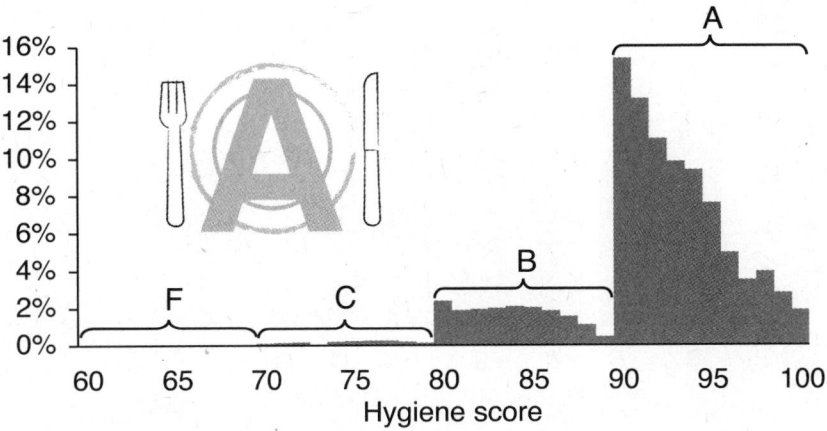

Figure 1-4. Distribution of restaurant hygiene scores.

The next example sticks to consumer safety but moves to the farming of marijuana. One significant challenge in this multibillion-dollar industry is that the humid growing conditions favorable to marijuana plants are also ideal for molds, some of which cause infections, dangerous immune responses, and even death. To protect the health of marijuana users, regulators have established limits on the concentration of molds and yeasts. However, in 2024, the *Wall Street Journal* obtained the lab results from several states and uncovered a very suspicious distribution, as shown in Figure 1-5. Most results showed mold levels just below the legal limit, with a sharp decline just above the legal limit. In a front-page story, the journalists concluded that the labs had underreported concentrations of molds, and that the system had failed to adequately detect hazardous mold in legal marijuana.

Let's conclude with another finance example. In the years leading up to the 2008 financial crisis, property values surged, prompting many property owners to refinance and cash out the increased value. This refinancing trend was arguably a key reason for why the subsequent drop in property values led to a wave of foreclosures and significant economic turmoil.

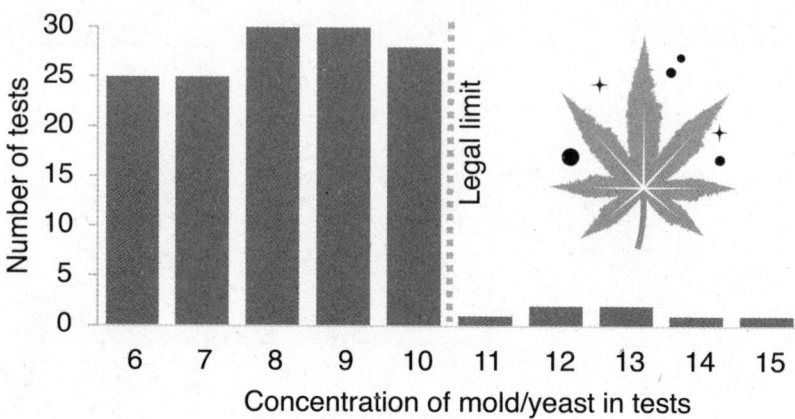

Figure 1-5. Test results of mold in marijuana.

To limit the risk for the lender, refinancings at attractive terms have maximum limits for the loan-to-value (LTV) ratio. The most critical cutoff is 80 percent, above which many lenders are unwilling to lend or borrowers are required to purchase mortgage insurance. Other relevant cutoffs generally come in increments of 5 percent.

Suppose you own a house worth about $300,000 with a $200,000 remaining mortgage. You hope to refinance to get a new loan with the maximum 80 percent LTV, meaning about .80 × $300,000 = $240,000, allowing you to cash out equity of $240,000 – $200,000 = $40,000. However, this hinges on the independent appraiser's assessment. What if you could inform the appraiser that you need a value of $300,000 to be able to complete the transaction? Would implicitly promising the appraiser more business in the future nudge them to arrive at a value of $300,000 or above? Such a quid pro quo arrangement is inherently corrupt.

Researchers John Griffin and Gonzalo Maturana examined the LTV ratio for hundreds of thousands of refinancing transactions before the financial crisis. Figure 1-6 shows the distribution of the LTV ratios for these transactions. A huge spike occurs at exactly 80 percent, with more moderate spikes occurring at 5 percent intervals, like 75 percent,

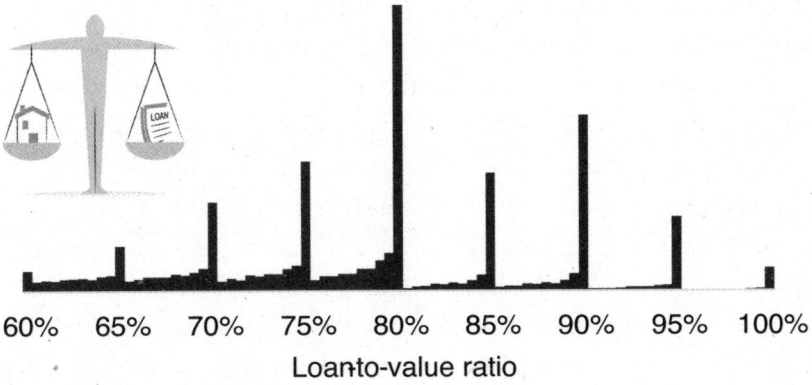

Figure 1-6. Distribution of loan-to-value ratios.

85 percent, and 90 percent. In contrast, there are hardly any transactions with an LTV ratio of, say, 81 percent. The spikes suggest that appraisers cater their assessments to meet their customers' needs.

One might argue that this pattern could arise for nonfraudulent reasons instead. For example, if an appraisal results in an LTV of 81 percent for the suggested loan amount, the lender and borrower might simply decide to lower the loan amount to achieve an LTV of exactly 80 percent. While this could explain part of the pattern, Griffin and Maturana also discovered that delinquency rates are abnormally high for loans with an LTV of 80 percent and other 5 percent increments. For example, the delinquency rate is higher for loans with an LTV of 80 percent compared to those with an LTV of 81 percent, 82 percent, and so on up to 89 percent, even though theoretically the latter loans should be riskier. This indicates that fraud is involved in a considerable portion of the loans with an LTV of 80 percent and other 5 percent increments.

Data Availability

Most of the data referenced in this book is publicly accessible, allowing anyone to explore vast amounts of information in search of suspicious patterns, with the ultimate goal of reducing fraud and corruption. Governments and various organizations routinely gather data for all kinds of purposes, and the public can often access it for free or at a modest cost. For instance, SEC's EDGAR website provides insider trading data and corporate filings like financial statements.

Since 1967, the Freedom of Information Act (FOIA) has granted the public the right to request information from the federal government and its agencies, with certain exemptions. Additionally, all states have their own freedom of information laws for state and local levels. These "sunshine laws" are crucial for providing journalists and scholars with access to data across various fields.

A good starting point is to submit a FOIA request to a government agency to obtain records of past FOIA requests (often referred to as a "meta-FOIA" request). This can help you understand what information has already been requested and disclosed, enabling you to formulate more precise and effective FOIA requests in the future. Some institutions, like the SEC, also provide information on their websites about recent FOIA requests and the data supplied in them.

2

Salami Slicing:
Collusion in the
Stock Market

And the parrot would say, with great rapidity, "Pieces of eight!
Pieces of eight! Pieces of eight!" till you wondered that it was not
out of breath, or till John threw his handkerchief over the cage.

—ROBERT LOUIS STEVENSON, *Treasure Island*

Interest calculations and paychecks are often rounded down to the nearest cent. In the penny shaving scheme, also known as *salami slicing*, a thieving computer programmer imperceptibly diverts the fractions of cents to a personal account. Over thousands or millions of transactions, these small slices add up to substantial sums. You might remember the scheme from movies such as *Superman III* and *Office Space*.

A few decades ago, a large group of stock dealers colluded to create their own salami slicing scheme by diverting chunks of stock transaction values to themselves. But at 12.5 cents for each share in a stock transaction, the slices were huge. The bold ploy persisted for years, making it one of the most profitable collusions in history.

The heroes in this chapter are two finance scholars who stumbled upon transactions data with missing slices. The discovery left them completely baffled, and some peers refused to believe such a brazen scheme could exist. This led to intense disagreements and the only

Figure 2-1. WrestleMania in academia.

WrestleMania match in academia, as depicted in Figure 2-1. But before we get there, you need a quick background into trading costs.

The Trading Costs

These days, buying and selling stock is super easy—just download an app, transfer some money, and start trading stocks alongside professionals on your smartphone. It is also seemingly very cheap. Robinhood Markets, Inc., entered the scene in 2015 with a flashy app, commission-free trading, and a mission to "provide everyone with access to the financial markets, not just the wealthy." By the end of 2019, all major brokerage firms, including Charles Schwab, TD Ameritrade, and E*TRADE, had eliminated their online commissions, saving retail investors $5 per stock trade or more. This was the culmination of a longer evolution. Back in the 1980s, you might have paid $40 plus 1 percent of the trade value for small trades. In the 1970s, it would easily have cost $100 or more to make a single stock trade.

But there is another cost lurking beneath the surface: the *bid-ask spread*, or just *spread* for short. The spread is the difference between the *bid* price that a professional stock dealer (or *market maker*, to use a fancy term) is willing to pay for a stock and the *ask* price that the dealer charges for the same stock. Thus, if the price is $47.68–92, a retail investor can buy the stock at the ask price of $47.92 but only gets the bid price of $47.68 when selling it.

In this example, the spread is $47.92 – $47.68 = $0.24, or about 0.5 percent of the average of the bid and ask prices. If you buy the stock for the long term, this might not be that big of a deal. But if you trade frequently, the spread gradually erodes any possibility of a decent investment return (unless you're an unusually gifted trader, in which case you should become a professional). Day trading, which involves many trades every day, is certainly a doomed endeavor in the presence of spreads of this magnitude.

What is the typical spread size then? The short answer: it depends. For the large-cap stocks in the S&P 500, there's so much trading that the spread is pushed down to less than 0.1 percent. But for the small-cap stocks in the Russell 2000 where the average market capitalization is a couple billion dollars, it is usually higher than 0.5 percent, and spreads of 1 percent to 2 percent are not unusual. The spreads are also radically higher during the first fifteen to thirty minutes of trading when traders are still jittery after their morning coffee.[1] So don't believe Robinhood's hype of "democratizing finance for all." Trading firms like Citadel Securities are making billions of dollars trading stocks for small investors at Robinhood, and you'd be wise to play the proven buy-and-hold game when investing in the stock market.[2]

As upset as you might be now, you should know that, like brokerage commissions, the spreads used to be much higher and the system even more rigged against small investors. One reason was the lower *liquidity* (how easily a stock can be traded at fair prices) and antiquated trading system of the past. Another reason was collusion among dealers.

The Spanish Silver Dollar and Stock Exchanges

The colonists in British North America did not mint their own money. Instead, they used foreign coins, most commonly the Spanish silver dollar. The Spanish silver dollar was often cut into eight equal pieces, hence the name "piece of eight," each of which had a value of a *real*. The coin's milled edge made it tricky to shave off some silver in the cutting process without being detected.

The practice of splitting coins into eight pieces likely influenced the New York Stock Exchange (NYSE) when it opened more than two hundred years ago, as stocks were traded in eighths of dollars. It wasn't until January 2000 that the NYSE adopted decimalization, allowing stocks to be traded in dollars and cents.[3] Shortly thereafter, the SEC required other US exchanges to follow suit by April 2001, leading NASDAQ to also convert to decimalization.[4]

Besides creating a headache for those of us who are used to decimalization, trading in eighths affected the spread. Specifically, because dealers want to make money on their trades, the minimum spread when trading with eighths was, well, one eighth. For example, a dealer might be willing to buy a stock at $12 and sell it at $12⅛. The spread could, in turn, adversely affect the stock liquidity.

At NASDAQ, the focus of this chapter, each stock has several dealers who compete to trade. The dealers continuously post prices at which they're willing to buy and sell the stock, and the spread in the prices is meant to compensate dealers for taking risk and committing capital. If you want to trade a stock, you would contact your broker, who, in turn, would contact a dealer who would complete the transaction via this competitive process. At the time that NASDAQ stocks traded in eighths of dollars, the competition between dealers should have driven the quoted spread down to one eighth for the most actively traded stocks, such as Apple. That should have left plenty of profits for NASDAQ dealers. Yet, as we'll see, they reached for more.

Two Scholars Stumble into the Arena

In the early 1990s, newly minted PhDs and assistant finance professors Bill Christie at Vanderbilt University and Paul Schultz at Ohio State University obtained a comprehensive data set of dealer quotes and actual trading prices for forty large NASDAQ stocks for a thirty-nine-day period in 1991. They intended to investigate patterns in spreads, the behavior of dealers, and the information content in dealer quotes. But before getting far on their original research idea, they detected a peculiar pattern in their data: there were almost no one-eighth spreads for Apple and most of the stocks in their sample. Upon closer inspection, they observed that the stocks were mostly quoted in even-eighths (meaning whole prices and quarters—prices ending in $^2/_8$, $^4/_8$, and $^6/_8$), whereas the odd-eighth quotes (meaning prices ending in $^1/_8$, $^3/_8$, $^5/_8$, and $^7/_8$) were mysteriously missing from the distribution. This observation contradicted their expectation that the quotes should be evenly distributed across even and odd quotes.

If dealers only used even eighths, the minimum spread would be $^2/_8$, or 25 cents, which would significantly harm investors. For instance, if an investor spent $10,000 to buy 250 shares of Apple at $40 and then sold them immediately, the sales proceeds would be 25 cents less per share, totaling 250 × $39.75 = $9,937.50. In other words, the quick round-trip cost $62.50, or a little more than $30 each way, which is double what it would have been with odd-eighth quotes and likely several times what it would have been with decimalization. Even investors who buy and hold for a long period to minimize trading costs are affected. For those investors, the $30 is money that could have been spent on buying more shares and would have compounded in value. Given that Apple stock has increased in value by more than five hundred times since the early 1990s, the investor, while very wealthy now, still lost out on more than $30 × 500 = $15,000.

Christie and Schultz were flabbergasted by the missing odd-eighth quotes. They thought there was a mistake somewhere, so they double-checked their data and their computer programs. They found no mistakes or errors. "My hands were shaking," Christie later told a reporter. "We were completely surprised," Schultz said. "Shocked, actually."

They abandoned their original research idea in pursuit of a deeper exploration of the peculiar data pattern, aiming to uncover the underlying explanation. They identified one hundred of the most active NASDAQ stocks in 1991. As a benchmark, they also identified one hundred stocks that traded on the NYSE or AMEX and had a similar size as their sample of NASDAQ stocks. Then they compared the distribution of quotes and the magnitudes of the spreads.

Figure 2-2 shows the distribution of quotes across the possible eighths. Clearly, the NASDAQ stocks had far more even-eighth quotes (85 percent of the total quotes) than odd-eighth quotes (15 percent of the total quotes). As an extreme outlier, Apple had 98 percent even-eighth quotes and only 2 percent odd-eighth quotes! In comparison, the NYSE/AMEX stocks had a fairly even distribution of quotes across even eighths (54 percent) and odd eighths (46 percent).[5] Naturally, the absence of odd-eighth quotes on NASDAQ significantly inflated the spreads and contributed to much higher trading costs.

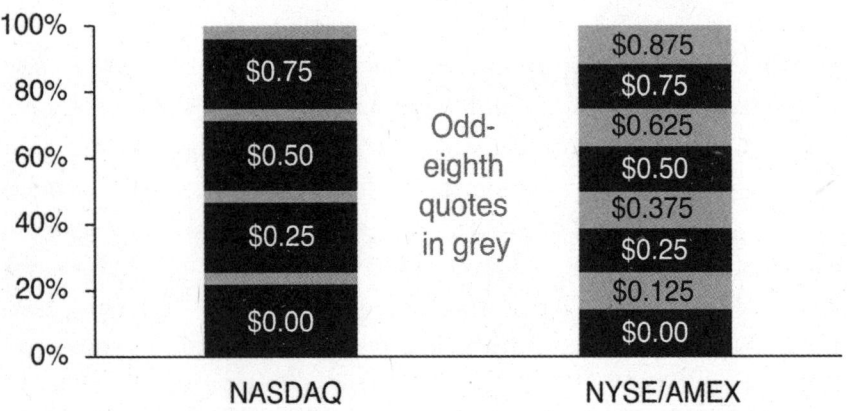

Figure 2-2. Distributions of even- and odd-eighth quotes for NASDAQ versus NYSE/AMEX.

What explained the absence of odd-eighth quotes among the NASDAQ stocks and the correspondingly higher spreads? After considering several possibilities, including structural features of the NASDAQ market, Christie and Schultz concluded that NASDAQ dealers must have colluded to avoid one-eighth quotes, thereby inflating the spreads and their profits. In particular, they wrote the following:

> *We believe that this surprising result reflects an implicit agreement among market makers to avoid using odd-eighths in quoting bid and ask prices and that a large number of market makers per stock is not necessarily synonymous with competition....*
>
> *We are unable to envision any scenario in which 40 to 60 dealers who are competing for order flow would simultaneously and consistently avoid using odd-eighth quotes without an implicit agreement to post quotes only on the even price fractions.*

In early 1994, the *Journal of Finance* accepted the research report for publication. The title of the published study was "Why do NASDAQ Market Makers Avoid Odd-Eighth Quotes?" The title originally included the word *collusion*, but a journal referee thought it was too strong for an academic publication.

Encouraged by a colleague, Christie and Schultz issued a press release about their research on May 24, 1994. Although they were excited about their results, as academics often are, they expected limited media interest, which is the norm for finance research.

The *Los Angeles Times* was the only major news outlet to contact the two researchers. It published a story on May 26, 1994, causing other reporters to ask for copies of the research report and publish their own stories. The ball started to roll. Many lawyers also requested the research report, a sure sign of looming legal battles. Christie feared that even he and Schultz might be targets of such a battle, but that fear turned out to be unwarranted.

The Response of the National Association of Securities Dealers

On the day of Christie and Schultz's press release, the National Association of Securities Dealers (NASD), which runs NASDAQ, summoned
a closed-door meeting of major market makers. At the meeting, NASD
chief operating officer Richard Ketchum expressed concerns about a
regulatory crackdown and suggested that some of the spreads should
be narrowed.

Publicly, NASD officials disputed Christie and Schultz's conclusions.
Ketchum argued that trades often occur between the quoted bid and ask
prices. In a letter to Christie dated May 31, NASDAQ president Joseph
Hardiman wrote that the research study "simplistically focuses only on
spreads, which both market professionals and knowledgeable academi-
cians understand to be but one component of transaction costs. Other
factors include liquidity and commissions charged to investors."

NASDAQ traders also tried to diminish the study. Said Nelson Gold,
head NASDAQ trader at Interstate Johnson-Lane: "Just because somebody
doesn't make a market in eighths, ergo everybody is colluding? Where is it
written that someone has to price stocks in quarters or eighths?"

Christie and Schultz Tighten Their Grip

Christie and Schultz recognized that the sudden media attention
around their original study offered a unique opportunity for a follow-up
study. They teamed up with PhD student Jeff Harris to examine how the
publicity affected the use of odd-eighth quotes and the magnitude of
the bid-ask spreads. They found evidence that the publicity had pro-
found effects.

As noted earlier, the *LA Times* first reported on Christie and Schultz's
findings on May 26, 1994, followed by the *Wall Street Journal* and other
outlets the next day. During the days immediately before the media
reports, nearly all of the almost sixty NASDAQ dealers of Apple stock
avoided odd-eighths when quoting Apple bid and ask prices. However,

within a couple of days of the media reports, all dealers used odd-eighth quotes—in fact, most of them used odd-eighth quotes more than 40 percent of the time. Figure 2-3 shows that, around the same days, the fraction of one-eighth spreads (the narrowest possible spread) increased from 0 percent to about 80 to 90 percent! This dramatic shift could not be a coincidence and made it significantly cheaper for investors to trade in Apple shares.

Based on their findings, Christie, Harris, and Schultz concluded that "our evidence suggests that spreads narrowed because an implicit agreement among market makers to maintain spreads of at least $0.25 was abandoned." In other words, their new results strengthened the conclusion of the original study that NASDAQ dealers had colluded to avoid odd-eighth quotes, and that media publicity from the first study had at least partially halted this collusion.

The *Journal of Finance* swiftly accepted the research report for publication. In a rare move, the editors expedited the publication process so that the follow-up study ended up in the same December 1994 issue as the original study.

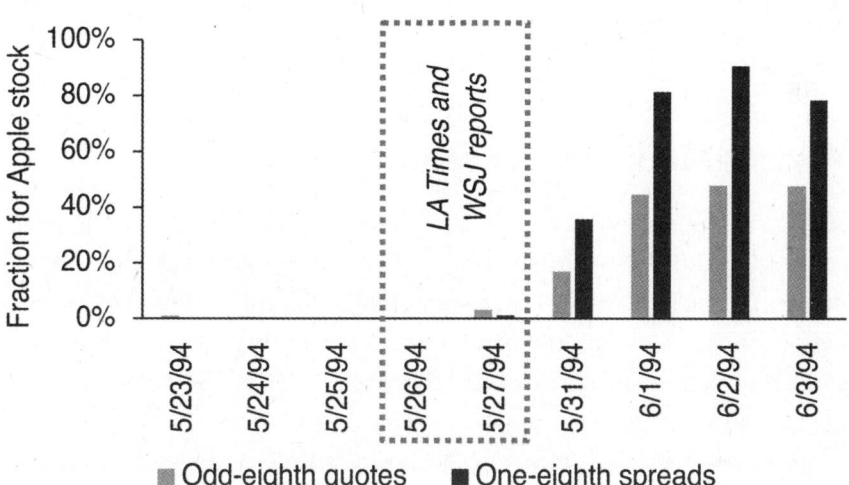

Figure 2-3. The effect of news articles on odd-eighth quotes and spreads for Apple stock.

Class Action Lawsuits and Other Investigations

In the aftermath of the media attention on Christie and Schultz's research, more than two dozen class action suits were filed in which major NASDAQ market makers were accused of collusion and price fixing, in violation of antitrust, federal racketeering, and securities fraud laws. The plaintiffs included the State of Louisiana on behalf of investors in the state, and the defendants included Merrill Lynch, Goldman Sachs, and Bear Stearns.[6]

Major plaintiff firms, including Milberg Weiss, entered the fray. While jockeying for position, Milberg Weiss retained Schultz as an expert. On the other side, the Wall Street firms retained an army of defense lawyers to fight back. Lawyers from both sides attended a luncheon in New York sponsored by analysts, during which Christie and Schultz discussed their research. Incidentally, Christie declined to work for either side and explained: "I'm agnostic about the lawsuits. I can't judge the legal issues. It was certainly not the reason we wrote the paper."

In October 1994, the US Justice Department and the SEC also got involved. A spokesperson for the Justice Department stated that "the antitrust division is looking at the possibility of anticompetitive practices in the (NASDAQ) stock market."

WrestleMania in Academia

Merton Miller served as an advisor at the University of Chicago to both Schultz (PhD '88) and Christie (PhD '89) and won the Nobel Prize in Economics (along with Harry Markowitz and Bill Sharpe) in 1990. He is most famous for his contribution to corporate finance, including—with Franco Modigliani—the Modigliani-Miller theorem, which states that firms' capital structure is irrelevant in a world without taxes and distress costs.

In the mid-1980s, Miller and Sanford Grossman wrote a theoretical paper titled "Liquidity and Market Structure" (published in the *Journal of Finance* in 1988) that was related to some aspects of Christie and

Schultz's research. For example, Miller and Grossman argued that "the currently quoted spread cannot serve any transactor as a precise measure of the cost of trading immediately rather than delaying the order." Miller later stated to a reporter that "I was a little ticked off with Christie and Schultz—my students—that they didn't even know our article."

When the NASD hired the Chicago-based economic consulting firm Lexecon to rebut Christie and Schultz's research, Lexecon, in turn, reached out to Miller and Grossman for assistance. Lexecon's vice president was a friend of both Miller and Grossman and was familiar with their past work. Miller later stated: "A lot of people think, gee, when they hire an economist, he'll say anything they want. No, no, no. That's not the way it works. You hire an economist because you know pretty much where he stands."

Miller and Grossman soundly rejected Christie and Schultz's collusion conclusion. They argued that price clustering, in which prices are quoted in round numbers, naturally occurs in many financial markets. Even in the housing market, listing prices, offer prices, and transaction prices tend to be rounded to thousands of dollars, even though in theory pennies could be used. They also argued that NASDAQ was highly competitive and collusion unlikely. The paper was presented at an academic conference at Vanderbilt in April 1995 hosted by Hans Stoll (a senior colleague of Christie and another former student of Miller), along with a couple of other studies that challenged Christie and Schultz's interpretation of the lack of odd eighths in the price quotes. The conference was confrontational, so much so that the local newspaper dubbed it "WrestleMania." I picture the researchers fighting in the ring, with plaintiff and defense lawyers cheering for their favorites, each with a financial stake in the outcome.

Legal Settlements and Outcomes

The Justice Department investigation revealed "substantial evidence of coercion and other misconduct" in the NASDAQ market. Anne Bingaman, the assistant attorney general in charge of the department's antitrust division, argued that NASDAQ traders who defied the convention of quoting prices in quarters were coerced and harassed. As one piece of evidence, she offered the transcript of a tape between two traders:

Trader A: He's trading in one-eighths and he's embarrassing your firm.

Trader B: I understand.

Trader A: You know, I would tell him to straighten up his act, stop being a moron!

In July 1996, the Justice Department settled a civil antitrust suit with twenty-four securities firms, including Goldman Sachs, Merrill Lynch, and Morgan Stanley. As is commonly the case in such settlements, the firms neither admitted nor denied guilt. The settlement barred the firms from engaging in collusive pricing practices on NASDAQ and required them to enhance compliance by recording and monitoring their traders' conversations.

In August 1996, the SEC reported that the NASD had failed to properly control NASDAQ.

In November 1998, a class action suit by investors (more than one million individuals and institutions who bought or sold shares between May 1989 and May 24, 1994) was settled for a record $1.03 billion, or $2 billion in 2025 dollars. Again, the Wall Street firms denied any wrongdoing, but they agreed to pony up. The lawyers got $143 million, a handsome payday for them earned through hard work, as indicated by three million pages of documents, ten thousand hours of audiotapes, and more than two hundred depositions.

The billion-dollar settlement proved to be an enormous task to implement. To receive a payment, investors had to have traded in one of the 1,659 NASDAQ stocks. More than 1.6 million claims were filed, 85 percent of which came from institutional investors. Individual investors received about 2.47 cents a share, while institutional investors, who were more likely to have transacted inside the spread, received a little less at 1.65 cents a share. The payment checks ranged from a paltry $25 to millions of dollars.

Harvey Houtkin, the so-called father of day trading and a pioneer in SOES (Small-Order Execution System) trading on NASDAQ, which involves making rapid buy and sell orders to profit from slight price changes, argued that NASDAQ dealers had swindled investors for far more than the record settlement indicated: "The industry dodged a major bullet. They got away with murder. The settlement is a joke. It wasn't even pocket change to the big firms. If they were forced to return some of their ill-gotten gains, the settlement would be hundreds of times what they paid out."

Aftermath

Despite the academic quarrels, the American Finance Association (the publisher of the *Journal of Finance*) awarded Christie and Schultz the Smith Breeden Prize in January 1996 for their original NASDAQ study. This is one of the most prestigious prizes, if not *the* most prestigious prize, that a research paper in finance can win.

However, there was backlash. Academic research in the fields of economics and finance depends heavily upon support from private and public sources. Leading up to Christie and Schultz's original study, the NASD contributed $10,000 annually for research at Vanderbilt's Owen School of Management. Christie said that the support ended in 1994.

I met Bill Christie for the first time when I visited Vanderbilt to present a paper in late 2003. At the time, he was serving as the dean of the business school. A very charismatic individual, he was more eager to show me a table-sized mechanical contraption in his office indicating where the sun was currently lighting up the globe (something I now have an app for on my phone) than to discuss the NASDAQ collusion.

3

The Midnight Maneuver:
Late Trading in Mutual Funds

Wall Street, with its army of brokers, analysts, and advisers funneling trillions of dollars into mutual funds, hedge funds, and private equity funds, is an elaborate fraud.

—MICHAEL LEWIS, bestselling author

While the New York Stock Exchange's closing bell at 4:00 p.m. marks the official end of each trading day, information never sleeps. Fresh data—including earnings releases, economic reports from Asia, and merger announcements—continues to pour in after hours. For most investors, this creates a frustrating wait until markets reopen. But for some privileged traders, this gap becomes an opportunity for exploitation.

Late trading is the financial world's version of a midnight heist, where a select few exploit the system to their advantage, leaving ordinary investors in the dark. And as with any heist, there are secret arrangements and rule violations along the way.

But there is a sheriff in town. As the attorney general of New York, Eliot Spitzer was eager to tackle the shenanigans, as Figure 3-1 illustrates. And he was willing to create enemies in the process, which he did, and it cost him dearly.

Figure 3-1. Eliot Spitzer as the Sheriff of Wall Street.

The Sheriff of Wall Street

Aided by major campaign contributions from his father, forty-year-old Eliot Spitzer was elected to be New York's attorney general in 1999. Spitzer quickly adopted a high profile by aggressively and publicly chasing white-collar crime. Because Wall Street was under the attorney general's jurisdiction, the financial services industry became a natural target for him.

Spitzer's first offensive on Wall Street culminated in a $1.4 billion "global settlement" with the ten largest investment banks on Wall Street at the end of 2002. As part of the settlement, investment banks were required to sever ties between analysts and investment bankers to reduce widespread conflicts of interest.[1] Furthermore, banks would end *IPO spinning*, a shady practice in which investment banks offer underpriced initial public offering shares to third-party executives in exchange for future investment banking business.

In October 2002, the CBS news program *60 Minutes* dubbed Spitzer the "Sheriff of Wall Street," and a couple of months later, *Time* magazine named him "Crusader of the Year." Spitzer was on track for big things, perhaps even the presidency of the United States.

In spring 2003, Spitzer was on the hunt for new targets. David Brown, a recent addition to Spitzer's team, came across an academic article revealing that mutual funds were swindling small investors by charging exorbitant fees amounting to billions of dollars annually. This discovery provided Spitzer's team with the target they needed. Now, they just had to find the right angle.

Mutual Fund Trading Games

Before we proceed, I need to introduce you to mutual funds and mutual fund trading. Mutual funds pool money from investors to purchase a portfolio of securities, such as stocks and bonds. These funds are then divided into shares that are sold to outside investors. By purchasing a share in a mutual fund, you effectively own a portion of each security within the fund. It's like getting a slice of a multilayered cake without having to buy the separate ingredients and bake it yourself.

The portfolio managers decide which securities the mutual fund should buy and sell, aiming to maximize its performance and outperform other portfolios with comparable risk. The mutual fund investors pay a fee, sometimes up to a couple percent of their investment value, for the portfolio managers' efforts. This fee obviously eats into the investors' overall return. Many investors argue that mutual fund fees are excessive, especially given the lack of clear evidence that portfolio managers consistently pick winning stocks and thus "earn their keep."

Jack Bogle, the late founder of Vanguard and an outspoken opponent of high investment fees, stated that "the mutual fund industry has been built, in a sense, on witchcraft."

The high mutual fund fees were the first issue that Spitzer's team identified. But at least those fees are transparent to investors. The more troubling issue that Spitzer's team stumbled upon relates to how mutual fund values are updated and traded. To understand, we need to dive deeper into the institutional details.

The value of individual mutual fund shares changes continuously during and outside trading hours. However, the *reported* value of these shares, the net asset value (NAV), is only computed at the end of each trading day based on the closing prices of all the securities in the mutual fund. And, importantly, any buy or sale of the mutual fund shares is based on the NAV.

By now, you probably recognize that the NAV is a snapshot frozen in time, quickly rendered obsolete by the continuous news flow. Savvy investors certainly do. After the market closes, information relevant to individual stocks keeps coming. In fact, many firms deliberately delay major announcements, such as earnings and merger announcements, until after trading hours. Furthermore, markets around the world have different trading hours. When the NYSE closes at 4:00 p.m., there are only a few hours until the Tokyo Stock Exchange (TSE) opens, followed by the exchanges in Shanghai and Hong Kong. The trading values at these exchanges provide investors with clues about the updated values of the mutual funds.

However, the *forward pricing rule*, established in 1940, prevents even the savviest investors from exploiting their updated valuations of the mutual funds. Specifically, any order to buy or sell mutual fund shares cannot be completed until the next time the NAV is calculated, ensuring that no one can trade based on outdated NAVs.[2] But what if the forward pricing rule were to be violated? Well, hold that thought for a few paragraphs.

As you've just learned, the shelf-life of NAVs is shorter than that of freshly made guacamole. (Sorry, my love for avocados made it hard to resist the analogy.) Another weakness is that the NAV might be out-dated even at the time that it's calculated because it might be based on outdated security prices. There are a couple of reasons for this. First, the securities might be infrequently traded, making updated transaction prices unavailable. Second, some securities trade during different hours than the mutual fund. For example, because the London Stock Exchange (LSE) closes several hours before the NYSE, a mutual fund trading on the NYSE that contains British securities might have to base its NAV on the earlier closing prices from the LSE.

Some investors exploit that stale prices are used to estimate the NAV in a trading strategy known as *market timing*. (This is a bit tricky, so hang in there for a couple of paragraphs until we get to the much simpler *late trading* strategy.) For example, if favorable market developments occur between the closing of the LSE and the NYSE, investors might place orders to buy mutual funds with British stocks shortly before the NYSE closes. In this scenario, the NAV falls below the true mutual fund value, because the NAV is based on the closing prices of the British stocks, which would have been higher had the LSE closed at the same time as the NYSE. Chances are very good, though not certain, that the next day's NAV will be notably higher than the current day's NAV, because it will reflect the uptick in the British stock values at the end of the current day's trading at the NYSE. Thus, investors can sell the next day with the expectation of collecting a nice profit.

While market timing per se is legal, mutual fund managers recognize that the profits of investors who engage in this practice come at the expense of those of their long-term mutual fund investors. Thus, many mutual funds have abolished the practice by instating redemption fees and limiting the number of in-and-out trades in a year to, say, four.[3]

Late trading is an especially egregious and illegal extension of market timing. Under the forward pricing rule mentioned earlier, mutual fund orders placed after closing at 4:00 p.m. should be filled at next day's NAV. However, some mutual funds treat 4:00 p.m. as a soft cutoff time, allowing brokers extra time to total the orders of the day before reporting them. This quickly becomes a slippery slope. If mutual funds provide too much leeway in how late an order can be and still be filled at the NAV of the day, the system becomes susceptible to abuse.

When would you expect late trading to be most lucrative? Naturally, the longer you can trade after closing, the better. A higher fraction of stocks traded in the Asian markets is also better. For instance, the TSE provides high-quality updates when it opens at 8:00 p.m. EST. If Japanese stocks surge after opening, you should buy shares in mutual funds with many Japanese stocks, assuming you can do so at the obsolete NAV. Thus, the Asian exposure supercharges our late trading profits. Keep a mental note of this until we see some empirical results at the end of the chapter.

The Whistleblower

As a young lifeguard on Long Island, Noreen Harrington learned to blow the whistle on unsafe behavior. Years later, she would blow the whistle again on the behavior she witnessed among her colleagues on Wall Street.

In 2003, Harrington worked for Eddie Stern, whose father, New York business magnate Leonard Stern, donated $30 million to New York University in the late 1980s to have its business school named after him. Eddie's hedge fund, Canary Capital Management, specialized in trading shares of mutual funds. When working late one evening in 2002, Harrington observed the Canary team gather around a computer terminal and celebrate some trades. Because this occurred well after trading hours, Harrington became suspicious and wary. She discovered later that Canary traders often placed orders between 4:00 and 8:00 p.m. Her questions about the trades were not welcome, and she left the Stern family business by Labor Day 2002, before fully understanding the curious trading activity taking place after the market closed.

In her next job, with a small investment firm, Harrington further investigated the after-hours trading until she better understood how some mutual funds permitted certain investment firms to trade at the NAV after it was set. Aware of Spitzer's assault on Wall Street, she mustered the courage by June 2003 to call Spitzer's office. She first left an anonymous message:

> I think you should investigate mutual funds. People are doing way too many trades and doing late trading after the close of business. There are violations of security laws by the hedge funds and mutual funds.

She followed up with another call, after which she agreed to be questioned by Brown and others on Spitzer's team who understood the mutual fund industry.[4]

The Canary Sings

At Spitzer's office, Brown assigned several law school interns to corroborate Harrington's claim. When an intern in Spitzer's office searched the internet for leads on market timing, he soon discovered a wealth of relevant information circulating in mutual fund chat rooms. Some of the chatter pointed to the Canary fund, and several of the incriminating posts were made by James Nesfield, who worked for Canary from home in North Carolina through his consulting firm Nesfield Capital, charging merely (at least by Wall Street standards) fifty dollars an hour.

Starting June 30, 2003, Brown contacted Nesfield and others affiliated with Canary with the threat of subpoenas. Brown quickly persuaded a nervous and broken Nesfield to cooperate, and on July 22, Nesfield drove his pickup truck full of documents to Spitzer's office. Nesfield also explained how he had assisted Canary. For example, he had searched for struggling mutual funds that faced large investor withdrawals, and then promised the mutual fund managers a large influx of capital in exchange for permission to make rapid trades in and out of their funds.

The day after, Andrew Goodwin, a former Canary portfolio manager, came to Spitzer's office to talk. The canary decided to sing. Eleven hours of interviews with Goodwin provided an astounding glimpse into Canary's market timing and late-trading operations.

Soon afterward, Spitzer's office was negotiating a deal with Eddie Stern. Spitzer aimed for a quick outcome and more ammunition so he could move on to other culprits in the industry. Stern eventually gave up the names of more than thirty funds that had given Canary special trading privileges; in return, Canary got what it viewed as a sweet deal: $40 million in fines.

How the Late Trading Was Conducted

What was in it for the mutual funds? Why did they allow certain investors the benefit of trading with hindsight hours after the NAV had been set? And how did the participants hide their tracks?

Mutual funds charge investors for the funds under management. Therefore, the larger the fund (in terms of the money invested), the more money the mutual fund makes and the more it can pay its managers. But attracting new capital can be tricky. A dirty shortcut is to allow some investors special privileges, like waiving redemption fees and allowing late trading, in return for parking money in the mutual fund. This shortcut might be particularly tempting for poorly performing funds that are bleeding money as investors make withdrawals.

Granting certain investors late-trading privileges proved to be an effective way for some mutual funds to improve the net inflow of funds. The additional fees generated for the mutual fund accrue to the mutual fund and its managers. But clearly, this is a zero-sum game in which someone must lose; the gain from late trading is effectively paid by long-term mutual fund investors who aren't privy to the arrangement, not by the fund itself and its managers.[5] Thus, it is easy to understand why the fund managers favor this arrangement and why they would want to keep it secret from their long-term investors.

Spitzer's investigation revealed that Canary negotiated with the managers of a Bank of America mutual fund to allow Canary to trade at the NAV of the day until 6:30 p.m. In return, Canary invested millions in Bank of America funds. In an alternate arrangement with Security Trust Company (STC), STC allowed Canary to trade until 9:00 p.m.

in return for a 1 percent fee on investments Canary made in the fund plus 4 percent of Canary's profits. By the time Spitzer targeted Canary, Canary had set up similar trading arrangements with at least thirty mutual funds.

Canary and other investors that engaged in late trading carefully covered their tracks. For example, Canary routinely called a complicit broker shortly before 4:00 p.m. with a list of proposed orders. The broker wrote the orders down on tickets and time-stamped them but did not yet submit them to the mutual funds. A few hours later, Canary would call again and inform the broker which orders to fully process and which to discard. That way, there was a paper trail of orders that were all seemingly placed before 4:00 p.m.

The Fallout

On September 3, 2003, Spitzer's office launched a broad attack, announcing that it had "obtained evidence of widespread illegal trading schemes, 'late trading' and 'market timing,' that potentially cost mutual fund shareholders billions of dollars annually" and that was "like allowing betting on a horse race after the horses have crossed the finish line." The pressure on the investment community persisted. The next day, the SEC, now collaborating with Spitzer's office, sent letters to eighty-eight mutual funds and thirty-four brokers, demanding that they surrender information related to late trading and market timing. Many of these came clean; at least one-quarter of the brokers admitted to having assisted with late trading, and half of the funds admitted to having permitted late trading via confidential arrangements.

Spitzer and the SEC instilled fear throughout the mutual fund world, triggering employee suspensions and confessions of improper trading activities in the hope of minimizing the damage. Yet Spitzer believed that the greater evil was the high mutual fund fees charged to small investors. Thus, in his negotiations with mutual funds, he sought to both punish and end unfair trading practices and lower the fees, even though the latter had not been part of the investigation and high fees are perfectly legal. For example, Alliance Capital agreed to pay $250 million in fines and restitution and reduce fees by 20 percent.

The settlements mostly took place in late 2003 and the beginning of 2004. By the end, the fines, restitution, and fee reductions totaled $3.6 billion. Over the following two decades, average fees have been more than halved as investors became increasingly aware of the impact of fees on returns and low-cost index funds proliferated.

Of course, Spitzer also put a large dent into unfair trading practices, the monetary value of which is less clear. The academic evidence, however, might shed some light on this.

The Large Sample Evidence

Finance researchers have repeatedly documented that a mutual fund's superior past performance does not increase the chance of superior future performance. However, investors believe otherwise and tend to invest more in funds with strong past performance.[6] As a result, if a mutual fund performs well one day, it attracts more funds starting the next day and continuing for weeks and months until the performance effect fades. In other words, there is a positive correlation between a fund's returns and subsequent inflow.

In contrast, it is unlikely that a mutual fund's inflow is correlated with its *future* performance; that would mean that mutual fund investors can predict which funds will outperform and invest accordingly. Now, I'm not completely dismissing the idea that some investors have a knack for picking winners. But let's be realistic: any scoop an investor has is likely about individual stocks, and the investor would be better off investing in those individual stocks than a mutual fund that owns a broader portfolio. So, we can agree that mutual fund inflow and *subsequent* performance should be uncorrelated, and that zero correlation is a benchmark for what is normal. If we notice any correlation, we should collectively raise our eyebrows.

Researcher Eric Zitzewitz collected data from 1998 to 2003 to estimate correlations between mutual fund performance and inflow for a study that was published in the *American Economic Review* in 2006. He did something clever that nobody else had done: he estimated the correlation between the inflow during a day and the mutual fund returns at separate time periods on the same day, including periods after closing when the inflow should have ended.

Figure 3-2 shows the correlations for each period. There is a strong and positive correlation between returns during the trading day and mutual fund inflow, especially for international equity funds. I find this a little surprising, but there might be an innocuous reason: some investors might recognize when a mutual fund is doing well even before it publishes the NAV and therefore buy some shares before the market closes.

Here's the shocker: the correlation persists for returns after 4:00 p.m. and extends all the way until 9:00 p.m. This is our cue to raise our eyebrows. How could the inflow, which supposedly ended at 4:00 p.m., be correlated with returns in the evening? Does this mean that we were wrong earlier, and that investors have a crystal ball that helps them buy before positive evening news? I'm not willing to accept that explanation. Instead, I believe that investors bought after the positive news, meaning that they kept buying after 4:00 p.m. and at least until 9:00 p.m. In other

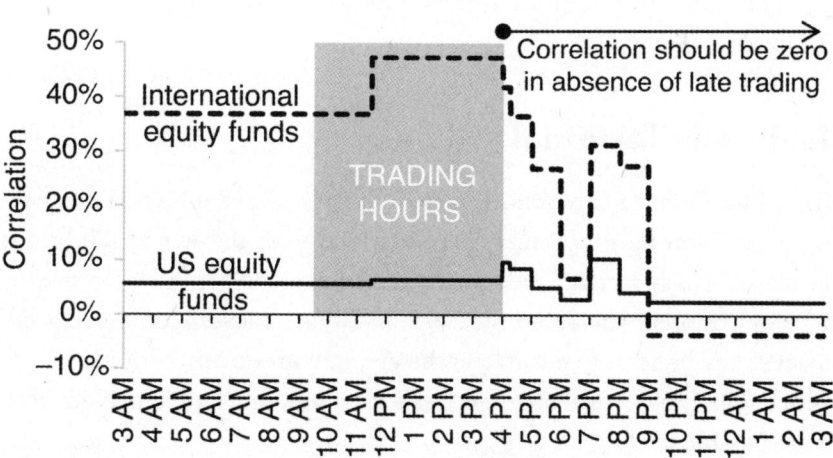

Figure 3-2. Correlation between daily fund inflow and returns for different intervals.

words, we're looking at evidence of trading late into the night that is recorded as an inflow that same day, in direct violation of the forward pricing rule that such trades should be completed at the end of the next trading day.

Seeing that this evidence is much stronger for the funds with international stocks than for funds with US stocks makes me even more convinced that late trading is the culprit. Remember I asked you to make a mental note earlier about how it's easier to profit from late trading in funds with Asian stocks, because the Asian stock markets give updated valuations when they open in the evening. Thus, I consider the case of the mysterious negative correlations after 4:00 p.m. to be closed.

Incidentally, the late trading must have been pervasive for the correlations to show up so strongly after 4:00 p.m. Had the late trading been sporadic in a few corners of Wall Street, it wouldn't feature so prominently in the data. Zitzewitz estimated that the annualized losses for long-term mutual fund investors from late trading totaled $400 million per year, or $700 million in today's value. While not trivial, it pales in comparison to other ways that long-term mutual fund investors are duped. For example, mutual fund fees are more than a hundred times the cost of late trading. But at least fees are legal. And some individuals (though not I) would argue that mutual fund investors get good value for the fees they pay.

Hubris Is Terminal

In a 2005 Harvard Law School speech, Spitzer said that he had received a T-shirt from an investment banker friend with the words "Hubris is terminal." These words would foreshadow events to come. Up until then, Spitzer's hubris had served him well. In 2006, he leveraged his success as attorney general to easily win the election for governor of New York, promising greater transparency and accountability at the New York state capitol.

However, the role of governor proved to be very different and more challenging for Spitzer than that of attorney general. His steamroller tactic prompted pushback from both Republicans and his fellow Democrats. In his first budget negotiations, he was forced to compromise on his goal of transparency and integrity by engaging in backroom talks and horse-trading to reach consensus.

Spitzer grew increasingly frustrated, especially with Republican State Senate Majority Leader Joe Bruno. During the summer of 2007, Spitzer's administration obtained information about Bruno's inappropriate use of the state aircraft and had state troopers spy on Bruno during his travels. The intel was then leaked to the press to damage Bruno politically. When details of the smear campaign emerged in the media, Spitzer became entangled in the scandal, which was dubbed Troopergate. The office of Attorney General Andrew Cuomo wrote a critical report of the Spitzer administration's behavior, leaving Spitzer with no choice but to apologize to Bruno.[7] Bruno then sought the assistance of Roger Stone, a self-described dirty trickster, to fight back. Stone resorted to his usual tactics to taint Spitzer and even left an infamous profanity-laced and threatening voice message for Spitzer's father.[8]

The worst was yet to come, however. Under the pseudonym George Fox, Spitzer had begun engaging with prostitutes from the high-end escort service the Emperors Club. He was obsessive about keeping this discreet, so much so that he instead stuck out, like when he was conspicuously hiding under a baseball cap at the Waldorf-Astoria Hotel on the way to meet a prostitute. He preferred to make payments that could not be traced to him, such as cash, but in a few cases, he wired money to offshore shell companies owned by the Emperors Club. As required by the Bank Secrecy Act to combat money laundering, North Fork Bank flagged some of the transactions as suspicious.[9]

Every day, thousands of transactions are reported as suspicious, so it is unclear why Spitzer's transactions would have attracted much attention. Supposedly, the IRS Criminal Investigation division first initiated a probe of the transactions based on the suspicion that Spitzer was a victim of identity theft or extortion, and the FBI got involved to investigate the possibility of political corruption, which eventually led to the Emperors Club. However, there are alternate theories for how Spitzer's indiscretions surfaced. Spitzer had created many powerful enemies with resources to investigate him. Moreover, Stone was still lurking with an outspoken agenda to take Spitzer down. Finally, Michael Garcia, the Republican US attorney for the Southern District of New York, held a grudge against Spitzer from previous encounters. Thus, the investigation of Spitzer might not have been so coincidental as it first seemed, and there appear to be some loose ends.

In January 2008, Garcia's prosecutors got permission to wiretap the Emperors Club and access its emails, an expensive and invasive step usually reserved for the most serious investigations. On February 13, they hit the jackpot with a wiretap of Spitzer meeting a prostitute in room 871 of the Mayflower Hotel in Washington, DC.

On March 6, the FBI arrested the managers of the Emperors Club. The accompanying affidavit submitted to the court and shared with the media was far more comprehensive than what arguably would be necessary for pure legal reasons. It described ten clients but focused mostly on Client 9, and it seemed intended to both humiliate Client 9 and allow the media to identify him by giving details such as the room number and date of the Mayflower wiretap.

Was this a political hit job? Garcia's office spent an unusual amount of resources to take down a small escort service. Moreover, it was uncommon for prosecutors to target customers, and in this case, they seemed to focus on just one. And then there was, of course, the affidavit that disgraced and all but revealed the identity of Client 9. Lastly, there were significant leaks to the press, ensuring swift identification of Spitzer as Client 9. All of this points to serious prosecutorial misconduct.

On March 10, the *New York Times* revealed that Spitzer had been caught in a wiretap with a prostitute. Spitzer apologized publicly the same day, and two days later, he resigned as governor. But despite a long and thorough investigation, he was never criminally charged.

The national and international press had a field day with Spitzer's downfall. He had fought hard for an image of high integrity and had even battled prostitution and escort services in his positions as attorney general and governor. Now, he was left as a hypocrite and laughingstock, garnering nicknames such as the "luv guv," "Eliot Mess," and "Client 9." Wrote the *Guardian*: "Rarely in American politics was a fall from grace so spectacular, so complete and so clearly down to a self-inflicted human flaw."

Epilogue

In May 2007, Spitzer and I briefly crossed paths. Given his reputation at the time as the Sheriff of Wall Street, *Time* magazine recruited him to write about my contribution to uncovering the scandal of executives backdating stock options. I remember thinking how memorable the article would be if Spitzer ascended to the presidency of the United States. I wrote a letter to thank him but heard nothing back. He understandably had other things on his mind.

4

The Mirage of Hedge Fund Performance

*The number one job of the hedge fund manager is
not to make sure that you can retire with a smile on
your face—it's for him to retire with a smile on his face.*

—MARK CUBAN, businessman and TV personality

When pitching its hedge fund in 2022, Twenty Acre Capital LP boasted a 2021 return of 44.8 percent. What it failed to specify was that this was the return for a single limited partner who had access to exclusive investments. The performance of the overall fund was sharply lower, at –5.7 percent. For this false advertising, the SEC ordered the fund to pay a $100,000 penalty in 2024.

In the high-stakes arena of hedge funds, where more than $5 trillion is in play, the temptation to present deceptive performance figures can be irresistible. More investors mean more of that sweet 2 percent management fee, even when the fund's actual performance is circling the drain. Top it off with the absence of pesky regulations, and conditions are ripe for fraud.

This chapter begins with background on the hedge fund world, but its main focus is the Bernie Madoff spectacle, of which most have heard but few understand. Perhaps the most interesting part of the Madoff fraud was not the amount of money involved, but the number of years

Figure 4-1. The collapse of Madoff's house of cards.

it persisted despite a row of highly visible red flags. He even claimed to defy financial gravity by producing high returns with little risk. Eventually gravity prevailed, causing Madoff's house of cards to collapse in a spectacular fashion (Figure 4-1).

The Hedge Fund Industry in a Nutshell

Hedge funds are the rock stars of the financial world, with flashy strategies and roller-coaster returns. Unlike their tamer cousins, mutual funds, hedge funds thrive on investing in exotic assets, confronting business executives, betting on market collapses, and levering up to amplify returns. For their efforts, hedge fund managers charge their investors heftily—the standard fee is 2 percent of the value and 20 percent of profits (commonly referred to as "2-and-20").

Rather than pursuing dull strategies that *hedge*, hedge fund managers constantly chase an investment *edge* to achieve outsize returns. The extra return they generate beyond appropriate benchmarks, such as the S&P 500 or funds with similar risk profiles, is known as *alpha*.[1] In fancy investment lingo, the pursuit of superior returns is referred to as "seeking alpha."

Alpha can be elusive, but hedge fund managers only need to convince potential investors of their special skills, because they get 2 percent of the asset value even when the fund loses money. Snake-oil salesmen figured out that general concept a long time ago—same con, fancier packaging.

To generate alpha, hedge funds need exceptionally gifted employees who can spot mispriced assets using publicly available information. Even better, they exploit insider information. Occasionally, they also actively engage with companies in their portfolio to enhance operations and unlock value. If hedge fund managers claim that they have some other secret sauce, I would stay away.

One skeptic of the hedge fund industry is Warren Buffett, the Oracle of Omaha. In 2008, Buffett challenged the hedge fund industry to a bet that a passive index fund strategy would outperform actively managed hedge funds. Protégé Partners LLC accepted a bet of a million dollars. Buffett easily won the bet: his index fund pick gained 126 percent, whereas the five hedge funds picked by Protégé Partners gained an average of only 36 percent.

Wall Street's Wild West

The hedge fund sector is the closest you get to the Wild West on Wall Street. Only the rich kids are allowed to play there, and no one cares if they get ripped off. Okay, that's a bit extreme, so let me clarify.

Hedge funds are only offered to "accredited" investors, meaning wealthy and supposedly sophisticated individuals. Regulators presume that these hedge fund investors can take care of themselves, so they grant hedge funds great operational flexibility and impose limited oversight.

One implication is that hedge funds use aggressive strategies like heavy leverage, short selling, and complex derivatives that are off-limits to traditional funds and much beyond the scope of this book. A fund could even bet everything on real estate in Cyprus or cryptocurrency.

The asymmetric payoff of the standard 2-and-20 compensation structure contributes to excessive risk-taking. That is, hedge fund managers get 20 percent of profits but are not penalized for losses. This means that a 50-50 bet on a gain of $100 or a loss of $200 gives hedge fund managers a 50 percent shot at a payday of 20 percent × $100 = $20, which they most likely prefer over a sure gain of $10, guaranteeing them only 20 percent × $10 = $2. In contrast, investors would be strongly opposed to the risky bet that is likely to result in a large loss for them, thus creating a clear conflict of interest.

Another implication is that hedge funds limit their disclosure on investment strategies and holdings. They might choose to report some of this information to appease investors and attract new ones. But the valuation of obscure and illiquid assets can be tricky and subjective, and hedge fund managers have incentives to skew the reports to deceive both current and prospective investors.

It also turns out that many of the investors in hedge funds are not really that rich or sophisticated. I've seen examples of older investors with a nest egg of a little more than a million dollars—sufficient to be considered an accredited investor—getting severely burnt on investments they did not understand at all. Additionally, there is a loophole for regular investors to indirectly invest in hedge funds—they can invest in *funds of funds*, which means that they invest in mutual funds that in turn invest in hedge funds. In that case, the mutual funds act as so-called feeder funds for the hedge funds.

The SEC has long acknowledged the significant potential for fraud in the hedge fund industry. To assist investors, it has developed a checklist, advising potential investors to first understand the fund's investment strategy, its use of leverage, any conflicts of interest, how the assets are valued, and how performance is determined. While this might sound reasonable, in practice, I doubt that even the SEC could fully grasp these complexities. So, the Wild West atmosphere triumphs.

Bernie Madoff, the $3 Billion Swindler

In 1960, Bernie Madoff began his business as a market maker on the fringes of Wall Street, matching buyers and sellers of small stocks. A few years later, he expanded into a side business as an investment advisor, managing small nest eggs from friends and relatives. To ease the burden of managing many small accounts, he pooled them together. This side business eventually laid the groundwork for his Ponzi scheme, while his trading business provided a veneer of legitimacy and cover, much like drug dealers operating a nightclub or restaurant to mask illegal activities and launder money.[2]

During the 1970s and 1980s, Madoff's trading business flourished. At that time, the typical spread between the ask price (at which investors could buy shares) and the bid price (at which investors could sell shares) was a hefty 12.5 cents, as discussed in Chapter 2. Acting as a middleman, Madoff would pocket this spread after facilitating trades between investors. To boost the volume of this business, he would "pay for order flow," offering brokers like Charles Schwab a cent or two per share to execute trades. Madoff is even credited with inventing this practice. Although such kickbacks are controversial and potentially unethical, they are not illegal, earning them the label "legalized bribery."[3] Madoff's brother also contributed by automating the trading process with computer technology. This strategy proved successful, and Madoff eventually became the largest dealer of NYSE-listed stocks.

Madoff's investment advisory business operated more discreetly. In November 1990, the investment firm Fairfield Greenwich Group started the Fairfield Sentry Limited Fund with $4 million for Madoff to manage. Over time, this fund came to be Madoff's largest feeder fund, with billions of dollars invested. But Madoff also used many other feeders, including the giant Spanish bank Banco Santander, which encouraged its customers throughout Latin America to invest in its Optimal fund. Common to them was that they were not allowed to list Madoff as an investment advisor, presumably because he lacked the proper license. Nonetheless, many insiders on Wall Street were aware of Madoff's involvement.

In addition to the feeder funds, some individuals invested directly with Madoff, including the "big four" of Jeffry Picower, Stanley Chais, Norman Levy, and Carl Shapiro. Madoff claimed that these four helped recruit customers for his business. If nothing else, they were treated differently than other investors and might have known about or been complicit in the scheme.

Highly uncommon for an investment advisor, Madoff charged no fee to his investors. He claimed that he made all the money on commissions in his trading business that supposedly handled all the trades for his investment advisory business.[4] Madoff's professed generosity should have been a glaring red flag for everyone to see. On Wall Street, there's no such thing as a free lunch. If he managed $5 billion that generated a 10 percent return annually, the standard 2-and-20 fee arrangement would have generated an annual fee of (2 percent × $5,000,000,000) + (20 percent × 10 percent × $5,000,000,000) = $200 million. Would he really give this up?

Another red flag was that the accountant for the investment advisory business was an obscure one-man operation in a strip mall about an hour's drive from New York City. If you run a squeaky-clean business, you should hire a reputable accounting firm that can validate your integrity.

In the early stages of his investment activities, Madoff claimed to make low-risk profits by taking simultaneous positions in an array of instruments that were mispriced in relation to one another. But such mispricings are rare and fleeting. An old riddle goes: What disappears as soon as you say its name? Answer: Silence. Similarly, once mispricings are discovered and acted upon, prices adjust, and the opportunity vanishes.

Later, Madoff's stated central investment strategy was a *split-strike* conversion strategy, also known as a *collar*. Let me try to explain. Madoff supposedly bought a basket of thirty to thirty-five of the stocks most correlated to the S&P 100 index. He then sold some of the upside to other investors by selling call options on the S&P 100 index or on the individual stocks in the basket and used the proceeds to buy insurance against downturns by buying put options.[5] This strategy resulted in a position that was less volatile than the S&P 100 index, yet retained some volatility by ensuring the strike price of the call options was higher than that of the put options, hence the name "split-strike."[6]

I apologize if I lost you along the way. The gist is that Madoff purportedly ended up with a stock position where extreme risk was removed. You should also know that diversified portfolios are subject to a fundamental finance law: with higher risk comes higher expected return, and vice versa. Consequently, as Madoff reduced the risk with his conversion strategy, the expected return of his portfolio should decrease correspondingly. Keep this in mind until we discuss his actual returns.

The fraud dates back to at least the early 1990s. Amid the prevailing recession, Madoff felt compelled to satisfy his clients' expectations at any cost. Consequently, he fabricated trades using stale prices, which was feasible because investors received statements of trading activity with a significant lag after they supposedly occurred. It is certainly easy to pick winning trades with perfect hindsight, and Madoff and his team were adept at making the trades appear legitimate on paper. As long as investors and regulators brushed the details aside and investors continued to invest with Madoff—why wouldn't they, given the impressive trades he reported?—Madoff was able to maintain his scheme.

In the late 1990s, the French aristocrat Rene-Thierry Magon de la Villehuchet, who managed the feeder fund Access International, informed Wall Street veteran Frank Casey about Madoff's investment advisory business and its impressive performance. Just how impressive? The best indicator is the reported performance of Fairfield Sentry's fund. Figure 4-2 shows the reported returns from December 1990 to October 2008 for Fairfield Sentry and the S&P 500 index as a benchmark. The S&P 500 index had sixty-seven months with losses that exceeded 1 percent, and three of those losses exceeded 10 percent. In comparison, Fairfield Sentry's worst monthly loss was only 0.6 percent! Despite the exceptionally low risk of Fairfield Sentry, it handily outperformed the S&P 500 index. Thus, Fairfield Sentry accomplished the remarkable feat of delivering a much stronger return than the S&P 500 index over a long period while taking minimal risk, in violation of the fundamental finance law noted earlier.

Was it possible for Madoff to generate such respectable returns while taking so little risk? Could his split-strike conversion strategy have worked miracles? If so, Frank Casey wanted in on this game, so he asked his colleague, Harry Markopolos, if he could figure out how it was done. After a quick analysis, Markopolos concluded that it could not be done and that it must have been a Ponzi scheme.

In May 2000, Markopolos submitted an eight-page memo to the SEC's Boston office, outlining his concerns about Madoff's business. He argued that Madoff's performance was simply too good to be true and that the purported strategy would have required more options than were available on the Chicago Board Options Exchange. Markopolos concluded that Madoff must either be front-running his order flow—buying stock for his investment business based on knowledge of his clients' orders in the trading business that would push the prices up—or running a Ponzi scheme, as his gut initially told him.

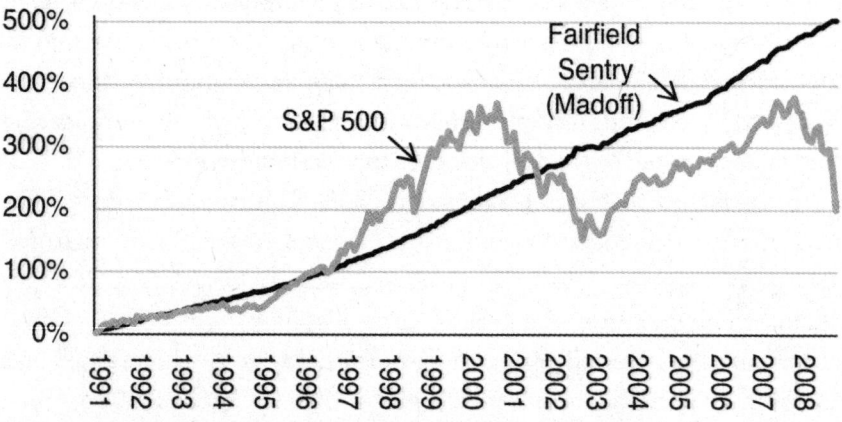

Figure 4-2. Performance of Fairfield Sentry and the S&P 500.

Markopolos even secured a meeting with an SEC enforcement lawyer. But he was unable to simplify and communicate his complex calculations demonstrating the impossibility of Madoff's returns. Lacking both investigative resources and an understanding of the alleged misconduct, the SEC failed to follow up with a thorough inquiry.[7]

In May 2001, Frank Casey contacted investigative reporter Michael Ocrant about the Madoff case. Ocrant was shocked to learn that Madoff managed so much money; he'd thought Madoff was just a market maker. The revelation was a story in itself. In his article "Madoff Tops Charts, Skeptics Ask How," printed in the industry publication *MARHedge*, Oscrant wrote:

> *What is striking to most observers is not so much the annual returns—which, though considered somewhat high for the strategy, could be attributed to the firm's market making and trade execution capabilities—but the ability to provide such smooth returns with so little volatility....*
>
> *In addition, experts ask why no one has been able to duplicate similar returns using the strategy and why other firms on Wall Street haven't become aware of the fund and its strategy and traded against it, as has happened so often in other cases; why Madoff Securities is willing to earn commissions off the trades but not set up a separate asset management division to offer hedge funds directly to investors and keep all the incentive fees for itself; or conversely, why it doesn't borrow the money from creditors, who are generally willing to provide leverage to a fully hedged portfolio of up to seven to one against capital at an interest rate of Libor-plus, and manage the funds on a proprietary basis.*

The weekly publication *Barron's* reiterated the concerns to a broader audience in an article called "Don't Ask, Don't Tell," in which the journalist Erin Arvedlund wrote:[8]

> *Still, some on Wall Street remain skeptical about how Madoff achieves such stunning double-digit returns using options alone. The recent MARHedge report, for example, cited more than a*

dozen hedge fund professionals, including current and former Madoff traders, who questioned why no one had been able to duplicate Madoff's returns using this strategy. Likewise, three option strategists at major investment banks told Barron's *they couldn't understand how Madoff churns out such numbers. Adds a former Madoff investor: "Anybody who's a seasoned hedge-fund investor knows the split-strike conversion is not the whole story. To take it at face value is a bit naïve."*

This prompted Fairfield Greenwich partner Jeffrey Tucker to attempt to verify Fairfield's supposed holdings of $3 billion. After Madoff presented fictitious trade records and phony trading programs meticulously crafted to look authentic even to an expert, Tucker was satisfied and did not ask for further verification. Even if Tucker did suspect fraud, it is unclear whether Fairfield Greenwich and other feeder funds had the incentive to sound the alarm, as they continued to collect hefty fees from their customers while Madoff stayed in business.

Although Fairfield Greenwich was content with the status quo, plenty of other investors stopped trusting Madoff with their money in the next couple of years. Some quietly withdrew their money, while others blacklisted Madoff. The SEC received more tips about Madoff in 2003, but the investigation was halted when resources had to be redirected toward allegations of mutual funds allowing investors to trade after the market closed, as discussed in Chapter 3.

By the fall of 2005, the SEC had received more letters of concern, including another report from Markopolos with the unambiguous title "The World's Largest Hedge Fund Is a Fraud." While Markopolos's arrogance and condescension rubbed many the wrong way, the report, combined with a subsequent meeting with Markopolos and various inconsistencies in Madoff's operations, alarmed some SEC employees enough to push for another investigation. Unfortunately, the SEC investigation that started in January 2006 was deficient and sloppy. When SEC lawyers visited Madoff in May 2006, Madoff was visibly irritable and nervous, but the SEC found "no evidence of fraud" and failed to follow up on several leads that would have uncovered the Ponzi scheme.

When the market collapsed in 2008, Madoff's fund was supposedly still up, so some investors, including Mr. de la Villehuchet, invested more money in his fund. But as the financial crisis continued, Madoff faced redemptions that he struggled to fulfill. Then his house of cards came tumbling down. In the beginning of December 2008, he confessed to his sons. On December 11, the FBI arrived at Madoff's door, and he admitted to the fraud. And on December 23, Mr. de la Villehuchet died by suicide after having invested $1.5 billion with Madoff on behalf of wealthy European clients.

Upon Madoff's collapse, SEC chairman Chris Cox conceded that "the Commission has learned that credible and specific allegations regarding Mr. Madoff's financial wrongdoing, going back to at least 1999, were repeatedly brought to the attention of SEC staff, but were never recommended to the Commission for action.... I am gravely concerned by the apparent multiple failures over at least a decade to thoroughly investigate these allegations."

Bernard Madoff received the maximum sentence of 150 years in prison and subsequently became estranged from his family. Tragically, one of his sons took his own life on December 11, 2010, exactly two years after Madoff's arrest. His other son passed away from cancer in 2014. Madoff himself died from chronic kidney disease on April 14, 2021.

The common belief is that Madoff's fraud added up to $65 billion. But most of this was just fictitious paper profits. Investors supplied around $18 billion, of which $15 billion was later recovered, mostly from investors who had withdrawn money in the years leading up to the collapse.[9] This suggests that the total loss was about $3 billion, not counting what this might have generated as returns elsewhere during the period that Madoff held it. Still a lot of money.

The Big Data Evidence

There were multiple strong clues of fraud in the Madoff case, including the secrecy around the investment advisory business, the lack of oversight and auditing, the absence of fees, and the strong performance relative to the low risk. Even then, it took decades for the fraud to be widely uncovered.

One might argue that it was difficult for outsiders to uncover the Madoff fraud in the early years. But eventually, the feeder funds had reported so many months of solid performance combined with low volatility that it should have been obvious that something wasn't adding up. The relationship between its solid performance and low volatility was so exceptional that it would be impossible to sustain it for a long period without cheating, either by using inside information (including front-running other traders, as noted earlier) or by reporting false values. If you saw someone win at the blackjack table again and again and again, wouldn't you start to get suspicious?

One might also suspect that many other hedge funds defraud investors by distorting the reported values. But it is unlikely that their fraud is as brazen as Madoff's or that the clues are as obvious. Nonetheless, with lots of reported data across thousands of hedge funds, we might see evidence of fraud.

The question is: What pattern should we be looking for as evidence of fraud? Hedge fund managers presumably have many goals, including beating the overall market and various benchmarks. If we observed hedge funds collectively beating the market and various benchmarks by a modest margin, that's not necessarily evidence of fraud; rather, it might reflect the managers' skill in picking high-performing investments.

Another goal of fund managers is to avoid losses, even small ones. Thus, they are likely to misreport slightly negative actual returns, as reporting positive returns would only require them to make small adjustments to some asset values. That is the premise of a study published in 2009 by Nick Bollen and Veronika Pool, who borrowed from the earnings management literature discussed in Chapter 5 to examine the distribution of reported monthly hedge fund returns in search of discontinuities around zero.

Figure 4-3 illustrates the study's main results, highlighting a clear discontinuity around zero. Specifically, there is a notably low frequency of reported returns right below zero (returns ranging from –0.20 percent

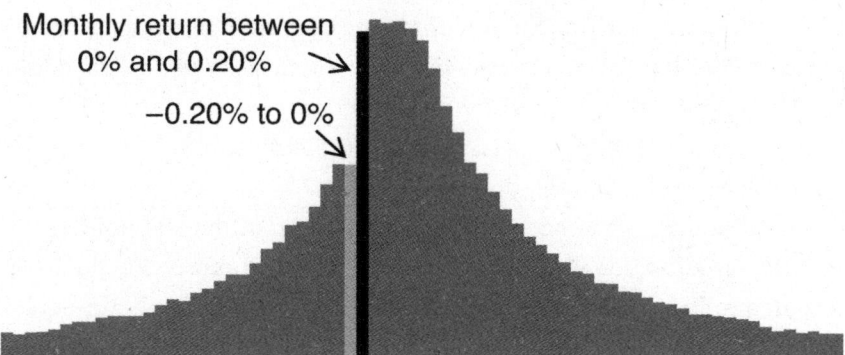

Figure 4-3. Distribution of monthly hedge fund returns.

to –0.01 percent) and a notably high frequency of reported returns right above zero (returns ranging from 0.01 percent to 0.20 percent). The most obvious explanation is that many hedge fund managers adjust slightly negative returns, perhaps by inflating the value of illiquid securities, to appear slightly positive instead.

Bollen and Pool's method effectively identifies adjustments that are common across many funds, such as minor tweaks to slightly negative returns. However, it falls short in detecting more significant discrepancies that vary widely among funds, like the example at the beginning of this chapter, where a true return of –5.7% was misreported as 44.8%. Thus, while their findings indicate that many funds regularly misreport, they do not reveal the most extreme cases of misreporting.

Avoiding Fraudulent Funds

In a follow-up study, Bollen and Pool suggested some unrelated possible indicators of fraudulent hedge funds.

One clue is that the reported hedge fund returns do not correlate with the returns on assets that are supposedly in the hedge fund portfolio. For instance, if a hedge fund claims to primarily hold stocks in the US stock market, its returns should closely align with indices such as the

S&P 500. If not, the hedge fund might be misreporting either its holdings or its returns. However, this clue has limitations, as hedge funds might hold a complex and proprietary mix of securities, including both long (buy) and short (sell) positions, making it difficult for outsiders to determine the expected correlations.

Another sign is the non-uniform distribution of the last digit of the reported returns. Ideally, about 10 percent of the digits should be 0, 10 percent should be 1, and so on, due to the random nature of actual hedge fund returns. If humans fabricate returns, they might favor certain digits or use copy-paste features, leading to a non-uniform distribution. This clue also has drawbacks: it requires a long series of returns to detect deviations from uniformity, and a savvy hedge fund manager could use a random number generator to produce returns with a uniform last digit distribution, thus avoiding suspicion.[10]

How, then, can you dodge fraudulent hedge funds? Personally, I steer clear of hedge funds altogether, and I recommend you do the same. However, if you choose to ignore this advice, you should critically evaluate whether the past or promised returns of the hedge fund seem too good to be true compared to other investments. If the returns are exceptionally high, ask yourself how the hedge fund achieves what others apparently cannot. And why is the hedge fund willing to share those exceptional returns with you? I suspect that you will not arrive at satisfactory answers, and that you will join my camp of hedge fund skeptics.

Interestingly, Madoff was aware of these concerns. Using reverse psychology, he created an impression of reluctance to accept new investors, fostering a sense of scarcity and exclusivity. Madoff would claim that the fund was closed to new investors. Similarly, about seven decades earlier, Charles Ponzi had encouraged investors to withdraw their funds from his scheme to build trust. It's like a grocery store offering an item on sale but limiting the quantity to two per customer; you're compelled to buy two—even if you only need one—because it must be such a good deal. Of course, Madoff would relent when investors pleaded for an exception. At that point, investors should have asked themselves: Why is Madoff willing to make an exception for me? What makes me so special? The harsh reality is that no one on Wall Street is inclined to share a truly good deal with anyone other than their closest friends and family members. Unconditional altruism is not a hallmark of Wall Street.

5

Financial Façades:
Earnings Management and Accounting Manipulation

Financial statements are like fine perfume;
to be sniffed but not swallowed.

—ABRAHAM BRILOFF, accounting scholar

When preparing to sell a house, the owners usually clean all visible surfaces and make minor repairs. They might even add a coat of paint and stage the home with stylish furniture. Similarly, when preparing to sell a car, the owner will vacuum, clean, wax, and buff out visible scratches. More questionable home-selling practices include painting over water stains, mold, and rot, and using air fresheners to mask the odor of mildew and dead rodents. For cars, dubious tactics include adding fluids to mask leaks, patching rust spots and holes with fiberglass and paint, and rolling back the odometer.

Common to many of these efforts is that they are merely cosmetic or temporary fixes intended to sell an illusion to prospective buyers. But a quick paint job can't get rid of the rot and rust hiding underneath. Eventually, someone will have to pay, and the cost might be higher than if the problems had been addressed properly in the first place.

Executives face similar incentives. Their firms are continuously on display for investors and lenders, placing a relentless pressure on executives to perform. To maintain a pristine façade, executives often engage in short-sighted behavior at the expense of long-term viability. And they might be getting some assistance from some unscrupulous accountants, perhaps like the punk accountants depicted in a classic *Far Side* comic with pencils pierced through their ears and noses and a tattoo reading "Add, Subtract & Die!" (The comic is worth looking up if you haven't seen it.)

This chapter exposes the tactics and tricks used to paint a rosier picture of a company's financial health. From creative accounting practices to outright manipulation, I'll uncover how some companies bend the rules to inflate profits and hide financial weaknesses. I'll also show when pervasive tactics come with large costs, such as when Ken Lay and Jeff Skilling ended up driving Enron off the cliff like Thelma and Louise, as illustrated in Figure 5-1.

Figure 5-1. Jeff Skilling and Ken Lay driving Enron off the cliff.

The Purpose of Financial Statements, and the Auditor's Dilemma

Accounting and financial statements, including income statements (where earnings reside) and balance sheets (where liabilities reside), serve several important purposes. Internally, firms use statements to help monitor operations and understand how and where they can make improvements. For this purpose, managers prefer the financial statements to be as accurate and complete as possible.

Externally, firms rely on financial statements to retain and attract capital. Bondholders, through covenants, and stockholders, through securities regulations, periodically require these statements to make informed lending and investment decisions.[1] Managers, therefore, aim for financial statements that are accurate, to enhance the firm's reputation with investors and comply with regulations, but also uplifting, to satisfy current investors and entice new ones. Can you see the tension here?

The auditor occupies a crucial position between the company and its investors, serving both parties but receiving fees only from the company. The auditor's primary responsibility is to review the financial statements and issue an opinion on whether the firm adheres to generally accepted accounting principles (GAAP). This role inherently involves a conflict of interest, leading to challenging dilemmas. On one hand, the auditor should conduct a thorough review and provide an unbiased opinion to establish and maintain a strong reputation within the investment community. On the other hand, the auditor must please their paying client, the company, to secure future business. As a result, we can't always trust that auditors will reveal their true opinion about the accuracy and completeness of the financial statements.

Why Executives Window-Dress Financial Statements

We all have façades in our lives—just think about how most people present themselves on social media, with pretty pictures of themselves partying with friends or dining at beachside restaurants at sunset, as if they live like worry-free and wealthy celebrities.

Similarly, corporate executives build façades around their companies, because it yields financial benefits to both the company and its executives. To better understand, it is useful to partition the discussion according to the two parts that executives commonly touch up: earnings and financial health. While a bit dry for non-accountants, it gets to the core of the culprits' motivation.

Ever since they attended business school, corporate executives have reiterated the goal of maximizing the stock price to enhance the wealth of the owners. This focus on stock price is reinforced with executive compensation packages that are tied to the stock price, ensuring that executives never take their eyes off the stock market. They also know that the most important driver of the stock price is earnings.

For simplicity, let's think of the stock price as the sum of all future earnings per share (EPS).[2] This means that having strong earnings today isn't sufficient; it's even more important for earnings to be strong in all future years. However, predicting future earnings is challenging, so it's common to extrapolate current earnings to forecast the future. This means that current earnings become the main determinant of the stock price, much like today's weather is the best predictor of the weather in coming days, unless you have access to a professional weather forecast.

In their quest to pump up the stock price, executives exploit investors' myopic perspective of focusing on current earnings. Specifically, executives "borrow" earnings from future periods to pad current earnings. If investors fail to recognize that reported earnings are partially borrowed from the future, the stock price will increase.

Let's consider an example of the impact of earnings management on the stock price. You'll even learn a simple valuation method for stocks as a bonus. Suppose a firm's true EPS is $2 and projected to grow at 5 percent annually. If other firms in the same industry have an average price-to-earnings (P/E) ratio (the ratio of the stock price to the EPS) of 20, you can argue that the firm should have the same ratio. Therefore, our straightforward stock valuation would be $2 × 20 = $40.

Now, suppose that executives privately inflate the EPS by $1, making it $3 instead of $2. This $1 must be "repaid" in future years, but we can disregard this repayment in our valuation because only insiders are aware of the "debt." Based on the higher EPS this year, investors mistakenly extrapolate future earnings to be higher. (They will surely be very upset when they realize that future earnings will actually be much lower with this scheme.) Using the P/E ratio, the updated stock price would be $3 × 20 = $60. So, with some deceptive finessing of the earnings, the executives were able to inflate the stock price by 50 percent, at least until outsiders discover that they've been duped.

Another crucial aspect to earnings is their classification into either recurring or non-recurring. *Recurring earnings* are earnings from the normal, ongoing operations of the firm, while *non-recurring earnings* are extraordinary and not expected to persist. Therefore, when investors extrapolate earnings to predict future earnings or value the stock based on the P/E approach, they rely on recurring earnings. However, distinguishing between recurring and non-recurring revenues and expenses can be challenging. For example, can we count on subscribers to renew their subscriptions next year? If so, we could classify subscription revenues as recurring; otherwise, they would be non-recurring. Executives aiming to maximize the short-term stock price might deliberately misclassify more of the revenues as recurring and more of the expenses as non-recurring.

Are you feeling like an accountant yet?

Now let's switch focus from pleasing stockholders to pleasing lenders. Managers aim to demonstrate robust financial health, particularly a strong ability to repay loans. Financial strength offers two major advantages for the firm. First, it allows the firm to borrow at a lower cost. Second, it enables the firm to borrow whenever it faces attractive investment opportunities or a liquidity crunch.

You might assume that lenders are always willing to lend toward profitable projects. Not so. Lenders are very narrow-minded in their lending decisions, focusing primarily on the company's ability to repay. This ability hinges more on the company's existing debt burden relative

to the value of its assets than on the prospect of new projects. Consequently, the company needs to keep its debt burden low enough so that
it can access the capital market whenever it needs funds for new projects and ongoing operations. Otherwise, it risks missing out on attractive investment opportunities or, worse, having to liquidate assets at
fire-sale prices. This explains why executives window-dress their companies' balance sheets.

How Executives Dress Up Financial Statements

Executives, with the help of their accountants and sometimes even
their auditors, have numerous ways to manipulate accounting numbers
and enhance the appearance of the firm's financial statements without
affecting actual operations. The accounting standards provide some
leeway to do this legally. Greater manipulation necessitates deviations
from the standards, which is treacherous, subjecting the company and
its executives to potential shareholder ire and lawsuits.

An accounting joke exemplifies the leeway. During interviews for an
accounting job, two candidates are asked what one plus one is. "Two,"
the first candidate answers. "What do you want it to be?" the second
candidate answers and is hired on the spot.

The most common objective of accounting manipulation is to boost
short-term earnings. Because earnings depend on both revenues and
expenses, managers look for ways to inflate reported revenues or lower
reported expenses. While they could fabricate numbers, they more commonly accelerate revenues from future periods or postpone expenses to
later periods.

Let's consider a couple of examples. Ordinarily, a company should
ship the products before recognizing (that is, recording and reporting)
the revenue. However, under so-called bill-and-hold sales, the seller
bills the customer and recognizes revenues, but continues to hold the
products. This arrangement is acceptable if the customer requests it,
perhaps due to a lack of storage space. But it is not acceptable if the
seller initiates the arrangement.

This appears to be what "Chainsaw Al" Dunlap (a nickname earned for his mass layoffs) did to inflate revenues as CEO of Sunbeam. Sunbeam persuaded retailers to buy grills months before they were needed in exchange for discounts. The grills were then stored at third-party warehouses leased by Sunbeam until the customers requested shipment.

Similarly, in 2016, Under Armour borrowed from future quarters to cover up slowing demand. At the end of each quarter, it pushed retailers to take its products early and redirected products intended for its factory stores to discount chains, thereby extending a remarkable twenty-six-quarter streak of 20 percent sales growth.

AOL, one of the major players in the early days of the internet with its famous "You've got mail" email alert, instead delayed expenses during its heavy growth in the 1990s. Until 1994, it treated solicitation costs for new customers (essentially marketing costs) as an operating expense, which seems very reasonable. However, starting in 1994, AOL started to treat these costs as an investment in assets creatively labeled "deferred membership acquisition costs." Not only does "investment" sound more appealing than "costs," but its drag on earnings is also spread out over time and effectively delayed.

Common to these strategies of recognizing revenues early or postponing expenses is that the managers effectively kick the can down the road, and the problems eventually return to haunt them. Consequently, either the managers must keep playing the game or the firms will suffer a hit to earnings. It is also possible, especially with external pressure from investors or regulators, that managers will admit to past irregularities and the firm will restate its former earnings. A new CEO might be particularly eager to undertake large restatements—often called a "big bath"—because they can blame the problems on past leadership and take credit for subsequent earnings improvements.

Another way to manipulate earnings is via *mark-to-market (MTM) accounting*, also known as *fair value accounting*. In traditional accounting, there's a clear distinction between accounting earnings and stock values: accounting earnings reflect the financial performance of the recent year, while stock values reflect future earnings. However, with

MTM accounting, this distinction fades, enabling firms to record the prospect of future earnings in the present.

An example illustrates the impact of MTM accounting. Suppose a firm has a subsidiary with EPS of $3 for the current year, a 50 percent increase from $2 last year. Further, suppose that the suitable P/E value is 25, meaning that the so-called fair value of each share in the subsidiary increased from $2 × 25 = $50 last year to $3 × 25 = $75 this year. What should the earnings contributed by the subsidiary be during the current year? The most obvious answer is $3 per share, and that's what traditional accounting would use. However, under MTM accounting, the subsidiary is treated as if it were a stock that increased in value by $25 per share, so the earnings per share instead becomes $25. I imagine that a conversation could go something like this:

Accountant: What was the earnings per share for your unit this year?

Manager of subsidiary: $3, up from $2 last year.

Accountant: Okay. That must mean that your unit increased in value. So let me do a quick valuation of that increase in value using some simple assumptions. If earnings continue to increase by 6 percent per year and our cost of capital is 10 percent, then the additional earnings can be valued as a growth perpetuity at $1 / (10 percent − 6 percent) = $25. That is also in line with a P/E ratio of 25 for the industry. So, I will report $25 as the earnings per share for you this year.

Manager of subsidiary: Can we do that? I got a little lost, but it seems like your calculation captures earnings for future years, not only the current year as I thought accounting should.

Accountant: We sure can, under mark-to-market accounting. In fact, if I wanted to, I could increase the growth assumption from 6 percent to 8 percent to double the earnings to $50. Easy, right?

In certain respects, MTM accounting is superior because it better reflects true value changes and is less shortsighted, capturing prospects beyond the current period. For those reasons, MTM accounting makes sense for financial assets with readily available market prices. However, it's less suitable for operating assets and financial assets for which market prices are not readily available, because someone would then have to estimate the values based on a set of assumptions and opinions. Therefore, the estimation is prone to subjectivity, error, and manipulation. For example, a manager seeking to manipulate the earnings upward under MTM accounting could simply use more optimistic assumptions in the valuation of the assets. Another issue arises when different firms in the same sector use different accounting techniques, or when firms use a mix of accounting techniques across their various operations. The mix of apples and oranges makes it difficult for outsiders to gauge true performance and accurately estimate firm values.

Managers might also aim to project financial strength and conceal financial weakness. Inflating earnings certainly helps in this regard. However, a significant obstacle is often a heavy debt burden. Enter *special-purpose vehicles* (SPVs), also called *special-purpose entities* (SPEs), which can hide both losses and loans like a magic wand.

An SPV is a subsidiary with its own assets and financial statements that is legally separate from the parent. A requirement to keep the SPV apart from the parent for accounting purposes is that a third party owns a substantial equity stake. The definition of a third party in this context is murky, while a substantial equity stake has been interpreted to mean at least 3 percent. With these lax requirements, it's easy for a company to move a portion of its assets and liabilities to a subsidiary and not consolidate that subsidiary's assets and liabilities into its own financial statements. Then—poof—a chunk of the company has disappeared, perhaps apart from some lingering clues in various footnotes to the parent's financial statements. It's as if the debt moved off the parent's balance sheet, thus the term *off-balance sheet financing*.[3]

There is no shortage of famous accounting mischiefs around the world, including Enron and WorldCom (which culminated in the two largest bankruptcies in US history at the time) and, more recently, the Chinese company Luckin Coffee, which also filed for bankruptcy. All three cases contributed to new legislation designed to protect US investors. The next sections focus on Enron and Luckin Coffee for variety.

I should emphasize, though, that earnings management doesn't cause financial difficulties but is often used to conceal them, which is why earnings management and bankruptcies often go hand in hand. Accountants are primarily messengers and should not be shot for this—except perhaps Arthur Andersen, which was likely complicit in the Enron and WorldCom cases.

Enron and Its Core Values

The fraud at Enron was so spectacular along multiple dimensions—including its size, the involvement of top executives, the excess compensation, and the ties to the Bush family and other high-profile politicians—that it spurred two best-selling books and a documentary. Ken Lay, Jeff Skilling, and Andy Fastow were arguably the primary culprits, but many others both inside and outside of Enron played supporting roles.

Until the late 1980s, the gas industry was heavily regulated, creating a low-risk environment that allowed gas companies like Enron to carry lots of debt. However, deregulation under the Reagan administration led to increased price volatility. This change spurred considerable demand for longer-term contracts from drillers and others who wanted to minimize volatility by locking in longer-term prices. Under the leadership of CEO Ken Lay, Enron promoted deregulation and thrived in this new market by acting as a middleman and charging a premium on longer-term contracts over predicted prices.

Amid the deregulatory turmoil, Lay sought outside assistance to better stake out the course of the business. This is how Jeff Skilling first came on board as a consultant for McKinsey in 1987. Skilling's impressive performance prompted Lay to hire him permanently a few years later to oversee Enron's trading operations. Skilling had one specific condition for joining: he wanted to use MTM accounting, the powerful earnings management tool.

As the market for exchange-traded contracts developed, driving down the profitability of middlemen like Enron, the company shifted to more complex option and swap contracts that were not traded on regular exchanges. In 1991, its board of directors and auditor, Arthur Andersen, approved the use of MTM accounting, and in January 1992, the SEC approved it for the trading operations.

The complexity of Enron's trading positions made them opaque and difficult to value, allowing the company to easily misstate the fair value of its positions and manipulate earnings under MTM accounting by adjusting these values. Moreover, Enron soon extended MTM accounting to other parts of the organization where the fair value was even more ambiguous, without any objections from its auditor or the SEC. This gave Enron free rein to report the earnings it desired. Coupled with the executives' obsession with the stock price, which was continuously displayed on screens throughout its headquarters, an explosive mix was brewing.

While Enron could control earnings under MTM accounting, its cash flow was insufficient to support its rapid growth, and Enron's heavy debt level made it challenging to maintain a high bond rating. Consequently, in the 1990s, Enron resorted to SPVs to hide its liabilities from its balance sheet. Although Enron guaranteed many of these with its own equity, making it clearly liable, it only had to disclose the guarantees in the footnotes. Moreover, to outsiders, these footnotes proved to be almost impossible to decipher.

Over the years, Enron, with the assistance and ingenuity of CFO Andy Fastow, accumulated hundreds of SPVs. Many of these SPVs had clever acronyms, such as JEDI, and facilitated creative use of MTM accounting while concealing burdensome liabilities. The one I describe next is *Braveheart*, named after the movie in which Mel Gibson portrays a Scottish freedom warrior.

Skilling was the visionary at Enron. Following the company's success in trading energy, he proposed the idea of trading bandwidth for the emerging internet economy, essentially reallocating bandwidth to meet demand. However, this venture faced challenges, including the absence of proven switching technology and falling bandwidth prices. In 2000, Enron altered the course slightly and entered a joint venture with Blockbuster Video to deliver video-on-demand, a very exciting possibility seven years before Netflix started its streaming service. Enron would handle the bandwidth side, while Blockbuster would use its connections to secure licenses for movies and other content. Even though the venture failed to meet the 3 percent independent ownership requirement, Enron treated it as a separate SPV. Pilot projects were conducted in a few dozen apartments on the West Coast with servers in the basements, based on which Enron optimistically projected profits of more than $110 million. These projected profits were recorded as earnings immediately under MTM accounting. Never mind that the project turned out to be a failure and never generated any actual profits.

With the burst of the tech bubble around the turn of the century, Enron's precarious situation began to unravel. In early 2001, Lay stepped down as the CEO and Skilling took over. However, it soon became apparent that Skilling might not be up to the task. Famously, during a conference call with investors, a fund manager specializing in short selling (betting that the price will tank) remarked, "You're the only financial institution that cannot produce a balance sheet or cash flow statement with their earnings."[4] Skilling, who had been slipped a note indicating that the fund manager was a short seller aiming to drive down the stock price, replied sarcastically: "Well, thank you very much, we appreciate that ... a**hole."

By the time Skilling had served six months as the CEO, the share price had plummeted by 50 percent. Consequently, on August 14, 2001, Skilling resigned for "personal reasons," forfeiting a $20 million severance package, which many investors interpreted as a sign of deeper problems. This paved the way for Lay to return and attempt to revive the company. In a private meeting on August 22, Sherron Watkins, an Enron VP, expressed concern to Lay about questionable accounting practices. Arthur Andersen, the auditor, became anxious and suggested consolidating some offshore units into the balance sheet. The unraveling accelerated: on October 16, some partnerships were consolidated, leading to large losses; on October 19, the SEC announced investigations of partnerships; on November 8, Enron filed restatements with the SEC; on November 19, Enron said it tried to restructure its debt; and on November 27, Enron announced that it would suspend all non-essential payments. Finally, on December 2, 2001, Enron filed for the largest bankruptcy in history, only to be beaten by WorldCom's bankruptcy seven months later.

In January 2002, Arthur Andersen admitted to shredding tons of Enron-related paperwork as the SEC investigations began. Just a week later, Enron fired the firm as its auditor. By June 2002, Arthur Andersen was found guilty of obstructing justice, marking the beginning of the end for the company. Having signed off on the books for both Enron and WorldCom, its reputation was irreparably damaged, and customers fled. After all, what is an auditor with a bad reputation?

In the aftermath of Enron's collapse, more than thirty of its executives and employees were indicted, and many were jailed. Lay was found guilty of fraud but died before the sentencing. Skilling and Fastow were sentenced to twenty-four and six years in prison, respectively. But despite the large number of individuals and organizations involved, Lay and Skilling stand out in the public's eyes as the executives who drove Enron off the cliff.

Ironically, the four stated core values of Enron were *respect, integrity, communication, and excellence.* To remind myself and others, I bought a paper stock certificate of Enron while it was still possible. I framed it, and, as a satirical joke, added a plaque that reads: "Respect, Integrity, Communication, Excellence... Best wishes, Ken Lay." It still hangs in my office, but the students who visit don't give it much attention anymore. Even the largest frauds fade into history.

Luckin Coffee's Bitter Brew

Luckin Coffee, founded in 2017, quickly gained popularity in China with its technology-driven approach, focusing on mobile ordering, delivery, a network of strategically located stores, and affordable yet high-quality coffee. The company aggressively pursued expansion with the goal of dethroning Starbucks in the growing Chinese market.

In May 2019, Luckin successfully undertook an IPO, raising $650 million in new capital and achieving a valuation of $5 billion. Much of its funds came from the United States, and it was listed on NASDAQ to facilitate easy trading of Luckin stock by US investors. Undoubtedly, the capital market success was due to Luckin's tremendous revenue growth. However, what investors did not quite understand was how the company had managed to increase revenues so rapidly and how it would continue to do during the months after the IPO.

Luckin leveraged its app to distribute millions of vouchers for free coffee and coupons for steep discounts on subsequent purchases, bringing the price down to a third of that at Starbucks. Customers placed their orders electronically and paid with WeChat and Alipay, the dominant Chinese e-wallets, thus bypassing cashiers.

However, Luckin employees also exploited the setup to fabricate sales of more than $300 million in ways that made common fraudulent techniques seem innocent by comparison. The web of deceit was complex—in essence, fake customers bought vouchers that were later redeemed for fake orders. These fake customers were all linked to Luckin employees and included personal WeChat and Alipay accounts, four corporate customers that bought vouchers in bulk, and third-party shell companies. With the money from bulk sales, a fictitious employee made dubious payments of $140 million to purported suppliers of raw materials and delivery services.

In January 2020, a whistleblower's claims that revenues had been fabricated since Luckin's inception triggered an internal investigation. Shortly afterward, a US short seller aiming to drive down Luckin's stock price circulated a damaging report. Based on massive data, including eleven thousand hours of video footage at Luckin stores and twenty-five thousand customer receipts, the report concluded that much of the reported revenues must have been fabricated.

After another few months of volatile stock prices, Luckin came clean on April 2. The internal investigation confirmed major accounting irregularities, implicating the CEO and other executives. The fallout was swift and brutal. Luckin's stock plummeted 75 percent overnight, causing the market cap to drop from $12 billion to $4 billion. A couple of months later, it was delisted from NASDAQ. It also had to pay fines of $180 million to the SEC, $9 million to the Chinese market regulator, and $180 million to settle a class action lawsuit. Finally, in February 2021, the company hit rock bottom when it filed for bankruptcy in the United States.

Despite its severe accounting fraud and subsequent ripple effects, Luckin was able to restructure and emerge from bankruptcy in April 2022. Its annual revenues have since climbed to about $5 billion, a couple of billion ahead of Starbucks in the Chinese coffee market.

The Regulatory Responses

Following the collapse of Enron, numerous congressional committees, including the Senate Banking Committee led by Senator Paul Sarbanes, held hearings to investigate what happened and how to prevent similar incidents. Political momentum began to build to address issues like weak corporate governance and audit problems. However, it wasn't until the WorldCom scandal and other egregious cases that the momentum was strong enough to lead to new legislation. On July 30, 2002, President George W. Bush signed the Sarbanes-Oxley (SOX) Act into law as "the most far-reaching reforms of American business practices since the time of Franklin Delano Roosevelt."[5]

SOX is too extensive to describe fully here, so I will only mention some highlights. It established a "monitor of the monitors," the Public Company Accounting Oversight Board (PCAOB), to issue auditing standards, inspect auditors, and impose disciplinary actions. SOX further provides guidance to enhance corporate governance and shifts more responsibility to the stock exchanges and the SEC. The NYSE and NASDAQ stock exchanges introduced new requirements on the number of independent board members and the qualifications to serve on major committees, including the compensation and audit committees. No longer could celebrities like OJ Simpson serve on corporate audit committees. Meanwhile, the SEC mandated further disclosure about the board and its responsibilities and about executive compensation.

SOX also added several new audit requirements. The audit committee must be composed of only independent directors, and the committee chair should have expertise on GAAP and the like. And both the CEO and the CFO must certify that every accounting statement "fairly represents, in all material aspects, the financial condition and results of operations" of the firm.

The more recent Luckin Coffee scandal elevated tensions between Washington and Beijing, prompting American lawmakers to push for stricter oversight of Chinese companies listed on US stock exchanges. This led to the enactment of the Holding Foreign Companies Accountable Act, which President Trump signed into law in December 2020. The law requires foreign companies listed on US stock exchanges to allow the PCAOB to inspect their financial audits; otherwise, they risk being delisted.

Detecting Accounting Manipulation

Regardless of the type of accounting manipulation, it's difficult for outsiders to identify and untangle it. I've found that one sure sign of such manipulation and similar façade building is when CEOs grow boastful and invincible, as in the cases of Elizabeth Holmes and Markus Braun, both of whom adopted black turtlenecks during their tenure as CEOs to emulate the late Steve Jobs. (You might recall the illustration of them in the preface.)

The story of Elizabeth Holmes is well chronicled in numerous documentaries and John Carreyrou's best-seller *Bad Blood: Secrets and Lies in a Silicon Valley Startup*. Holmes founded Theranos, which claimed to have developed a portable blood-testing device that required only a droplet of blood from a finger prick to detect far more medical conditions than its competitors could. While Holmes aspired to develop such a device, she never succeeded and, thus, resorted to an array of techniques to deceive investors and journalists and filled her board with respected and well-connected individuals, like former secretary of state George Schultz (whose grandson was one of the whistleblowers), former secretary of state Henry Kissinger, former secretary of defense Bill Perry, and former Marine Corps general and later secretary of defense James

Mattis, to establish credibility and trust. For years, her façade held up, as she raised billions of dollars from investors and won numerous accolades, including being named among *Time* magazine's Most Influential People in the World. Theranos unraveled after Carreyrou received tips of the deception from insiders and wrote a series of exposés for the *Wall Street Journal*. Despite Holmes's aggressive tactics to hinder and discredit Carreyrou, she could not prevent her downfall, which included both civil lawsuits and criminal charges. In November 2022, she was sentenced to eleven years in prison.

Markus Braun, meanwhile, became a billionaire based on his vision of a cashless society and served as the CEO of the German payment giant Wirecard from 2002 to 2020. Wirecard and Braun's downfall began in January 2019, when the *Financial Times* raised concerns about the integrity of the accounting at one of Europe's rare technology success stories. Wirecard countered by accusing the *Financial Times* of corrupt reporting and hired the accounting firm KPMG to address the allegations of accounting irregularities. But KPMG received insufficient documentation to put the allegations to rest and reported in April 2020 that it could not "make a final judgment on whether the documentation and information are complete, correct and free of contradiction," causing Wirecard's stock price to plunge almost 30 percent. The final blow came in June 2020, when its longtime auditing firm, EY (formerly Ernst and Young), failed to verify Wirecard's reported bank balances of €1.9 billion and stated that the company had engaged in "an elaborate and sophisticated fraud." This caused Braun to resign, Wirecard to file for insolvency, and the company's $14 billion valuation to evaporate.[6] The Netflix documentary *Skandal! Bringing Down Wirecard* covers this demise in detail.

There are many indicators of earnings management beyond executive arrogance and black turtlenecks. A significant clue is when firms report earnings that just barely surpass certain benchmarks. These benchmarks include zero earnings (the threshold before turning to losses), the reported earnings from the previous period, analysts' forecasted earnings, and the earnings level that would trigger violations of loan covenants. When a firm's earnings are close to these benchmarks, the pressure on managers to deliver increases, and the temptation to cheat to meet or beat the benchmark intensifies.

Sometimes it is obvious why benchmarks matter. For example, if the board of directors has promised the CEO a bonus for meeting a certain earnings target, the CEO has a strong incentive to reach that target, but not necessarily more.[7]

Other times you might argue that some of these benchmarks are irrational. For example, is it that much worse for a firm to be slightly in the red than slightly in the black? Wouldn't a rational person consider the profit essentially zero in both cases? The field of behavioral economics has demonstrated that people, including managers and shareholders, can be quite irrational in such situations. The use of reference points, like zero earnings, is quite common. We often fixate on these reference points when evaluating performance, perceiving slightly positive earnings as significantly better than slightly negative earnings. In other words, losses loom larger than profits.

The retailing world discovered our tendency to use reference points a long time ago, which is why we often see prices like $1.99 instead of $2.00, as consumers instinctively read the former to be materially cheaper than the latter.[8] In a similar vein, many executives are preoccupied with reporting earnings growth from the prior period, even if the growth is minimal, because it shows an upward momentum. The prior earnings level is an especially important benchmark after a string of consecutive growth figures that managers wish to continue, perhaps as a talking point or a matter of pride. The only benchmark we've discussed that is of real consequence is the earnings level that triggers covenant violations, because covenant violations might, in turn, prompt creditors to interfere with the firm's operations.

Another indicator of accounting manipulation is that the firm is preparing to sell more of its equity. Whenever we sell something of significant value, we have an incentive to prop up its value. We've already discussed the superficial preparations people make before putting their car or house on the market. Similarly, managers window-dress their company before selling equity stakes.

Yet another sign of accounting fraud is when the reported earnings are much higher than the reported cash flow. It is akin to a friend boasting of a high salary but never seeming to have any money. Accountants call the difference between earnings and cash flow *accruals*, and they are wary when accruals increase. But just like your friend might simply spend the bulk of their salary to pay off old debts, there might be innocuous reasons for accruals. For example, toy manufacturers deliver many products to retailers before the holiday season but might not be paid until the beginning of the following year. In that case, they would record the revenues in one year, but the cash inflow would occur the next, giving rise to positive accruals in the fourth fiscal quarter of the year.

Finally, the Enron case has taught us to be guarded when firms use extensive MTM accounting, which managers use to manufacture earnings by changing some valuation assumptions, and extensive SPVs, which often conceal both losses and loans. At least some analysts should have discovered that Enron likely used these methods for deception purposes. For instance, it was highly suspicious that investment banks, eager for Enron's business, were willing to buy stakes in Enron's SPVs to meet the 3 percent independent ownership requirement. Moreover, several footnotes gave clues about the extensive use and structure of the SPVs.[9]

In summary, a skeptical examination of the financial statements and the accompanying footnotes, along with an understanding of external pressures to deliver certain earnings levels, can provide hints of mischief. Nonetheless, individual cases typically require inside information from an auditor or whistleblower to establish a good case and a complete understanding.

The Big Data Evidence

Despite the difficulty of detecting earnings management and other accounting manipulations in individual cases, analyses of large databases of financial statements have uncovered suspicious trends. Let's first review some of the managers' earnings objectives: achieving positive earnings to ensure they're "in the black" (because being "in the red," even slightly, is often seen as a failure); demonstrating positive earnings growth, which indicates positive momentum for the business; and meeting or beating analysts' earnings forecasts. These objectives might lead managers to inflate earnings, particularly when true earnings are slightly negative, exhibit slight negative growth, or fall slightly below analysts' forecasts. In each of these scenarios, even modest manipulation can "fix" the problem.

In a groundbreaking study published in 1997, David Burgstahler and Ilia Dichev displayed the distributions of earnings levels and changes for a large sample of US firms from 1976 to 1994. The distributions showed that the number of observations with earnings levels or earnings growth just below zero were conspicuously low. The only reasonable explanation for this is that managers who recognize that their earnings level or growth will be slightly negative for the year (or quarter) ask their accountants to make some last-minute modifications to push the earnings level or growth into positive territory. In short, earnings manipulation had occurred on a large scale.

Figure 5-2 replicates Burgstahler and Dichev's core results. It shows the distribution of earnings (return on assets, to be precise) for US firms, not including utilities and financial firms, from 2000 to 2020. Even for this later sample period, we can see a clear discontinuity around zero, with abnormally many observations at zero or slightly above, and abnormally few observations slightly below zero.

As an extension, I repeated the analysis using data for Chinese firms. The distribution for these firms shows an even stronger discontinuity around zero, with abnormally many observations at zero or slightly above. In addition, there are very few negative earnings in the sample; while about half of the earnings are negative among US firms, less than 10 percent of the earnings are negative among Chinese firms. This is highly suspicious, and I would take the reported earnings of Chinese firms with a grain of salt, especially if those earnings are barely positive.

In a 2022 study, Nadya Malenko, Joseph Grundfest, and Yao Shen used a similar methodology to document that firms nudge earnings

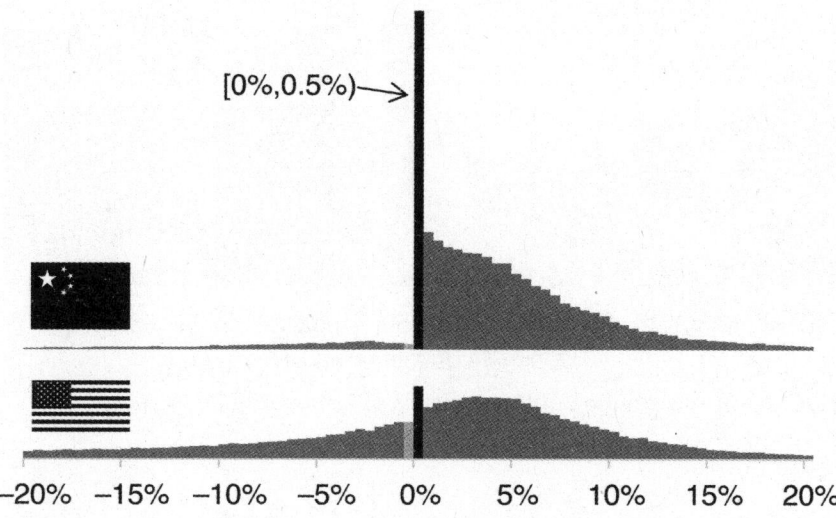

[0%,0.5%)→

−20% −15% −10% −5% 0% 5% 10% 15% 20%

Figure 5-2. Distributions of earnings for US and Chinese firms.

upward when their EPS are close to being rounded up to the next whole cent. Suppose that a firm's earnings divided by its number of shares is 32.46 cents, and that the firm reports the EPS in whole cents. That means that the reported EPS should be 32 cents. But it wouldn't take much to push the earnings up slightly so that the reported EPS ends up being rounded to 33 cents, and this seemingly trivial difference can have a significant effect on the stock market reaction. Indeed, when the researchers estimated the EPS in cents for a large sample of firms, they found that the number 4 is underrepresented in the first decimal of the estimated EPS. They also found that firms with conspicuous missing EPS estimates with a first decimal of 4 are linked to subsequent restatements of earnings, SEC enforcement actions, and class action lawsuits. I replicated their main result in Figure 5-3 based on firm data from 1980 to 2021, but using two decimals for the estimated EPS instead of one to get a more granular picture of the effect. As the estimated EPS get closer to the half-cent mark, there are markedly fewer observations, followed by a sharp reversal at exactly the half-cent mark, consistent with manipulation.

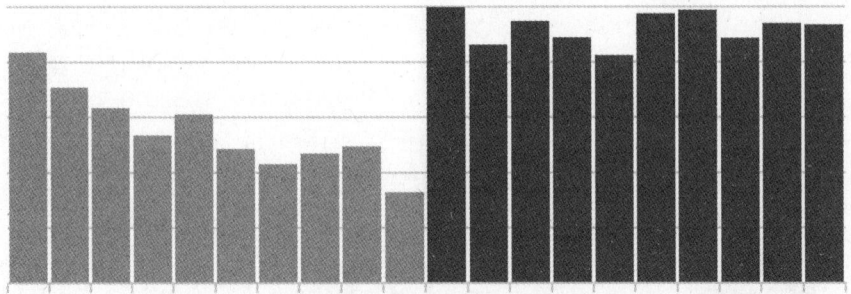

.40 .41 .42 .43 .44 .45 .46 .47 .48 .49 .50 .51 .52 .53 .54 .55 .56 .57 .58 .59
Decimals of estimated EPS

Figure 5-3. Distribution of the decimals of estimated EPS in cents.

Another set of studies has explored earnings management around specific corporate events, with one of the most examined being when companies sell shares to the public. Researchers have studied a couple of ways that firms inflate earnings before equity sales. One common method is known as *accruals management*, which involves manipulating earnings while keeping cash flow intact, resulting in a purely cosmetic effect. Such earnings management should manifest as positive accruals, where earnings exceed cash flow.

However, as noted earlier, positive or negative accruals might stem from legitimate business activities unrelated to earnings management. For instance, purchasing new machinery causes significant cash outflow yet only a minor reduction in earnings due to depreciation in the same year, thereby reducing the accruals. To remove such innocent effects on accruals, academic accountants have developed and refined algorithms that compare a firm's accruals with those of benchmark firms in similar situations. This comparison helps distinguish between *nondiscretionary accruals*, which are common among the benchmark firms, and *discretionary accruals*, which are more likely due to earnings manipulation. While this method is crude for individual companies, it seems to work quite well when averaged across many firms, as is common in research studies.

Researchers Daniel Cohen and Paul Zarowin observed a gradual increase in discretionary accruals during the years leading up to equity offerings. This trend suggests that firms engage in accruals management to present a more favorable image before selling new shares. Once the shares are sold, the discretionary accruals tend to revert toward zero, as the firms no longer need to enhance their financial appearance.

The second method firms use to inflate earnings before equity sales is known as *real earnings management*. This involves making operational changes that enhance the firm's short-term appearance at the expense of its long-term operations and value. Unlike the cosmetic earnings management techniques discussed earlier, real earnings management can be more destructive because it disrupts the operations of the firms. Many managers prefer it over accruals management, however, because it is less likely to violate accounting guidelines and trigger subsequent earnings restatements and lawsuits.

In their examination of real earnings management around equity sales, Cohen and Zarowin identified three subcategories. For simplicity, let's focus on only one here: the acceleration of revenues through greater price discounts and more lenient credit terms. The evidence shows that firms offer price discounts and more lenient terms to boost revenues in the year of the equity offering. This inflates earnings and might deceive potential buyers into paying a higher price for the shares. The other subcategories also indicate that firms engage in real earnings management before equity sales to temporarily boost the price, even if it might harm long-term operations and competitiveness.

Is it worthwhile for firms to engage in such behavior in the long term? Perhaps not. However, this decision lies with the executives, and by the time the long-term consequences become apparent, they might have already moved on, having collected their bonuses and cashed out their stock and stock options. Consequently, any cost is left to long-term stockholders. That includes you and me, as we hold stocks in our retirement accounts.

6

Insider Trading:
When Secrets
Pay Dividends

The most valuable commodity I know of is information.

—GORDON GEKKO, *Wall Street*

Daring traders on Wall Street actively seek privileged information to gain an edge and make their fortunes. However, this practice is fundamentally unfair to uninformed investors, undermines confidence in the financial markets, and can deter participation, making it more difficult for firms to raise capital.

This chapter explores the complex web of insider trading, examining some of the most notorious cases, including Martha Stewart's ImClone scandal and Raj Rajaratnam's South Asian insider trading ring. While both Stewart and Rajaratnam were convicted, most insider traders evade punishment. This includes billionaire Steve Cohen, depicted in Figure 6-1 as a distant puppet master of both his hedge fund traders and New York Mets baseball players, who escaped all but relatively minor consequences.

Figure 6-1. Steve Cohen as the puppet master.

The Allure of Illegal Insider Trading

Corporate insiders are allowed to trade stock in their own companies and often do so. But they are not allowed to trade on nonpublic information, such as knowledge of an imminent acquisition. Nor may they pass on that information to others, like friends and family members, for them to trade on and make a profit, especially if the insiders expect to receive something in return for the tip. Even the recipients of nonpublic information are in violation of securities laws if they use it to make trading profits.

Throughout this chapter, I'll refer to trading based on material non-public information as *illegal insider trading*, regardless of whether the perpetrator actually is an insider. In fact, corporate insiders are easy to identify and closely monitored, making it difficult for them to exploit private information for personal trading gains. Thus, most illegal insider trading is likely scattered among a myriad of anonymous shareholders who have obtained inside information through their personal network.

Ideally, the enforcement of insider trading laws levels the playing field on Wall Street, encouraging individuals from all walks of life to invest and making it easier and cheaper for companies to raise capital. Paradoxically, it also prevents prices from reflecting all available information, making trading on nonpublic information very profitable.

As discussed in Chapter 4, hedge funds and other players on Wall Street are continuously searching for an *edge* to generate *alpha* (superior returns). In some trading circles, *black edge* refers to inside information. The profitability of trading based on inside information makes it highly appealing for return-seeking investors, and many of them will add it to their investment arsenal.[1] The trick is to do it without leaving behind incriminating evidence that the SEC or other enforcement agencies can discover and act upon with their limited resources. This entails minimal written and oral communication that can be recorded or wiretapped, obfuscating trades and trading patterns, and maintaining a distance between the traders and the source of inside information.

One helpful vehicle for insider trading is so-called expert networks, like Gerson Lehrman Group (GLG), which are designed to facilitate communication between investors and experts in various fields. For example, an investor researching a pharmaceutical company might seek up-to-date information about certain diseases and treatment. The investor can contact GLG, which in turn will reach out to its vast expert network for someone with the required expertise.

According to a 2005 commentary in the *Journal of the American Medical Association*, GLG had contracts with more than sixty thousand physicians, each of whom charged between $200 and $1,000 per hour for consulting. Naturally, many of these physicians possess nonpublic information that could be of great value to investors. Although their contracts with GLG prohibit sharing such information, they undoubtedly slip up occasionally during lengthy conversations. These "slip ups" might even be deliberate, as they increase the value of the experts to investors and make the experts feel particularly helpful. My sense is that GLG prefers to just collect its cut and overlook these instances. In any event, GLG plays a central role in one of the insider trading cases discussed next.[2]

ImClone, Sam Waksal, and Martha Stewart, America's Homemaking Queen

In 1994, Sam Waksal and his younger brother, Harlan Waksal, founded the pharmaceutical company ImClone. Both brothers had tumultuous backgrounds. Sam had a history of cutting corners, which got him expelled from a Stanford lab, and he had been involved in numerous lawsuits and money disputes over the years. Meanwhile, Harlan had been caught in Florida in the 1980s for trying to smuggle two pounds of cocaine, but he avoided a long prison sentence because he had not consented to being searched. Nevertheless, the brothers steered the young company toward success in the coming years, and by 2001, ImClone had a promising cancer drug called Erbitux in the pipeline.

Sam Waksal lived extravagantly. He had a luxurious New York apartment filled with expensive art and surrounded himself with celebrities. An acquaintance described the people in Sam's life succinctly as "bimbos, intellects, art people, and investors." Sam was also a close friend of Martha Stewart, America's homemaking queen, and dated her daughter, Alexis. Martha Stewart bought a few thousand shares in ImClone, which would turn out to be a big mistake.

On September 19, 2001, ImClone announced that it had agreed to co-develop and co-promote Erbitux with Bristol Myers, and that Bristol Myers would buy a 20 percent stake in ImClone from existing shareholders at a price of $70, representing a 40 percent premium above ImClone's stock price of $50 the day before. ImClone's stock price shot up to $57 upon the news. By the beginning of December, the price had climbed above $70 in anticipation of Erbitux's approval by the Food and Drug Administration (FDA). Life was smiling at the Waksal brothers, but that was about to change.

On December 25, Harlan Waksal learned that the FDA almost certainly would reject ImClone's application for Erbitux due to insufficient data. Not wanting to spoil Christmas for his family, Harlan waited until the next day before passing on the bad news to Sam. The news put Sam in a bind. His extravagant lifestyle consumed substantial financial resources, and he had borrowed $50 million to buy ImClone stock on margin. So he swiftly initiated steps to sell his stock and instructed his family to follow suit. This seemed rather foolish, as Sam must have been aware that these sales would constitute illegal insider trading, and the SEC routinely flags large stock sales before announcements of bad news. Said US attorney James Comey (who, later as the head of the FBI, got tangled up in the 2016 Clinton-Trump fight for the US presidency): "It was incredibly dumb, obviously, to just try and dump that much stock on the eve of an important decision. It was like running around in your underwear, in broad daylight." Then again, Sam had engaged in crimes before, including forging the signature of ImClone's general counsel to obtain a bank loan and avoiding paying a million-dollar sales tax to the State of New York by shipping artwork to New Jersey.

Sam Waksal's family members managed to unload their shares. However, as an insider, Sam was subject to a blackout period for trading immediately before ImClone's public announcement, so even his attempt to first transfer the stock to his daughter before selling failed. This activity alerted Sam's broker at Merrill Lynch, Peter Bacanovic. Bacanovic did not necessarily know about the FDA decision, but he certainly understood that ImClone was in trouble. Despite multiple Merrill Lynch policies to keep such information to himself, Bacanovic decided to share it with one of his most important clients, Martha Stewart. Bacanovic and Stewart both had fathers of Eastern European origin and shared a passion for the Chow Chow dog breed, and they'd spent pleasant times together in Stewart's kitchen.

In the middle of the day on December 27, Stewart was en route to a coastal resort in Mexico, so Bacanovic simply left a message with Stewart's assistant that "ImClone is going to start trading downward." Stewart received the message when her plane landed in San Antonio for fuel, and this is likely when she called Bacanovic's office, as minutes later, all of her 3,928 ImClone shares had been sold at an average price of $58.43.

After the market closed the next day, ImClone announced the negative FDA decision. When the market reopened on Monday, December 31, ImClone's price dropped $9 (16 percent), and over the next week it dropped another $10. By selling when she did rather than on the day after the announcement, Stewart dodged losses of about $47,000. (She was later charged with avoided losses of $45,673.) Had she sold a few weeks later, her losses would have been larger yet, at about $100,000. Either way, it was pocket change for Stewart.

A week later, SEC lawyers questioned Bacanovic about the trades. Bacanovic spun a story that he had made an agreement with Stewart on December 20 to sell her ImClone shares if the price were to fall below $60. To support the story, he had scribbled "@60" on a worksheet that listed Stewart's ImClone holdings, but he used a different pen than the one he'd used elsewhere on the worksheet—an action that would have dire consequences for him. In an interview conducted by the FBI, SEC, and US Attorney's Office a month later, Stewart repeated the lie of a $60 agreement and claimed not to know about the Waksal sales when she sold her shares. But the investigators were skeptical that such an agreement was ever made. Why, for example, did Bacanovic not sell the shares as soon as the price fell below $60 around 11:00 a.m. on December 27? Instead, he waited for a couple of more hours, at which point the price had fallen below $59.

In June 2002, Waksal was arrested for insider trading. The case was clear-cut, and the following year, he was sentenced to more than seven years in prison for his misdeeds.

Stewart, meanwhile, maintained her innocence. Numerous experts argued that the case against her was weak and that most prosecutors would not have pursued it. Some even suggested that Stewart was being targeted as a highly successful woman—she was the first self-made female billionaire in American history—and that this was all a "bitch hunt."

On June 4, 2003, Stewart and Bacanovic were indicted on federal counts. James Comey announced that Stewart's "criminal case is about lying—lying to the FBI, lying to the SEC, and lying to investors." Immediately afterward, Stewart escalated her fight for innocence with a full-page ad in *USA Today* and a website. In February 2004, Stewart got some good news when the judge threw out the securities fraud count against her. But in March, she was convicted for conspiracy, obstruction of justice, and lying to a federal investigator. Bacanovic was only convicted for falsifying a document. In July, both were sentenced to five months in prison and five months of home detention. Stewart later said the prosecutors who put her in prison "should've been put in a Cuisinart and turned on high."

It is rare for a broker to get implicated in insider trading, and Bacanovic might have avoided prison had he not remained loyal to Stewart. Nonetheless, Stewart blamed him for her predicament, refused to assist him with his legal bills, and did not send him a Christmas card from prison. Bacanovic, in turn, blamed Stewart for not settling her charges, which might have led to better outcomes for both. He also blamed her for the loss of his identity—he was reduced to Stewart's broker and his fellow inmates just called him "Broker"—and was banned from the securities industry.

In 2006, Stewart settled a civil lawsuit with the SEC, agreeing to pay $195,801, which represented the losses avoided of $45,673, interest of $12,389, and a civil penalty of three times the losses avoided. Her larger financial loss, however, came from the fall in the stock price of Martha Stewart Living Omnimedia, in which she held 31 million shares. The stock price dropped about $10 due to Stewart's legal troubles and her inability to perform her duties in the company. Most notably, the price dropped more than $3 on the day she was convicted, even though the market had already punished the stock for a couple of years by then. Thus, we can conclude that Stewart's legal woes cost her hundreds of millions of dollars, and considering the continued decline in stock value, she probably lost more than a billion dollars in total. So much for trying to avoid a loss in only the tens of thousands.

In a final ironic twist, the FDA approved Erbitux in 2003. Had Stewart and Waksal postponed their sales until the middle of 2004, they might have fetched a sweet price of more than $80 per share.

I met Stewart at an event in New York City in 2007. By then, she had served her prison sentence and appeared radiant. Although I was tempted, I refrained from asking her about the ImClone case. She simply seemed eager to get on with her life as it was before her legal woes.

In 2024, Netflix released a much-hyped documentary about Martha Stewart. While it covers her entire life, it emphasizes the insider trading case as a pivotal moment in her illustrious career, one that punctured her once flawless façade. In a *New York Times* interview, she expressed frustration that the documentary dwells too much on the trial and prison sentence, which she now views as a vacation. But the documentary also shows how she has remained relevant in the new era of social media and shifting cultural landscape, such as by making TikToks with Snoop Dogg, whom she met during her edgy roast of Justin Bieber at Comedy Central. She has resurrected her façade, albeit with a fresh look.

A Billionaire Hedge Fund Manager, His Driven Employee, and a Brilliant Midwestern Medical Doctor

In 2002, Dr. Sid Gilman was a highly respected neurology researcher at the University of Michigan, so esteemed that a wing of the university hospital bore his name. He devoted most of his time to his research, especially after his oldest son had died by suicide two decades earlier and he'd become estranged with his surviving son. Then, one day, Gilman received a call that would take him down a dark path and forever stain his professional reputation, so much so that the University of Michigan ended up removing his name from the hospital wing and severed all ties with him.[3]

The call came from a GLG representative, inviting Gilman to join GLG's network of experts and earn $1,000 an hour by consulting with people from the investment community. With his $350,000 salary and modest lifestyle in Ann Arbor, Gilman had no need for money. But he signed on, if nothing else for some diversion. The resulting doubling of his salary was a bonus that allowed him a dash of luxury, like first-class plane tickets.

In mid-2006, Mathew Martoma, a portfolio manager at SAC Capital Advisors, contacted Gilman through GLG to learn more about Alzheimer remedies, specifically the experimental drug bapineuzumab, or bapi for short. Bapi, developed by the pharmaceutical companies Elan and Wyeth, had the potential to become a blockbuster drug, perhaps even surpassing Lipitor. As the chair of the safety committee overseeing the bapi clinical trial, Gilman was an expert on the drug and had regular access to patient updates. But he knew little about SAC Capital, a hedge fund run by the secretive billionaire Steve Cohen that was so successful that many assumed it was exploiting nonpublic information to gain a black edge. And Gilman certainly didn't know Martoma.

Martoma seemed to have it all. Polite, tall, and handsome, he had an undergraduate degree from Duke, where he had volunteered in the Alzheimer's wing of the Duke Medical Center, as well as an MBA from Stanford, where he met his wife, who was studying for her medical boards to practice medicine. However, his past had some blemishes. Harvard Law School had expelled him for forging transcripts.[4] Moreover, he was under immense pressure to prove himself at SAC. Thus, he worked long hours and became obsessed with bapi.

Gilman quickly took a liking to Martoma, whose brightness and inquisitiveness reminded Gilman of his deceased son. Over the next couple of years, Gilman and Martoma talked frequently, primarily on the phone but also at medical conferences, developing a sort of friendship or father-and-son relationship. The conversations, which could last for hours and for which Gilman was being paid handsomely, revolved around bapi and Alzheimer's but also digressed to family matters. To Gilman, Martoma seemed genuine, and Gilman wished to help Martoma however he could.

Although it violated GLG guidelines, Martoma asked Gilman many direct questions about the bapi study. Gilman strived not to share confidential information and would often answer questions in vague and theoretical terms. As Martoma persisted with his many inquiries, Gilman gradually lowered his guard and divulged confidential information, first accidentally and then more deliberately. At the same time, Martoma, despite his junior standing at SAC Capital, convinced Cohen to accumulate enormous positions in the stocks of Elan and Wyeth.

In 2008, Gilman was asked to present the most recent test results of bapi at the annual International Conference on Alzheimer's Disease to take place in late July in Chicago. Researchers from around the world would attend, and so would Wall Street analysts. In preparation for the presentation, Gilman received detailed test results and developed PowerPoint slides along with the Elan team. Notwithstanding the highly confidential nature of this information, Gilman shared the test results and slide content with Martoma. They spent more than an hour discussing the slides over the phone, and then Martoma traveled to Ann Arbor a couple of days later to personally review them.

The test results were not clear-cut, but Martoma viewed them to be worse than what Wall Street had expected. Martoma passed on the negative news to Cohen. Consequently, starting July 21, SAC Capital began secretly selling its shares in Elan and Wyeth and instead bet on a price decline by taking a large short position of 4.5 million Elan shares. When Gilman made his remarks on July 29, 2008, SAC Capital was perfectly positioned for the ensuing Elan and Wyeth stock price declines. By liquidating its Elan and Wyeth positions and then shorting the stocks, SAC made an estimated $276 million, for which Martoma received a $9 million bonus.

After the conference, Martoma abruptly cut ties with Gilman, leaving him confused. Earlier that year, Gilman had been diagnosed with lymphoma and was recovering from chemotherapy. Martoma had previously shown great concern for Gilman's health, but now he would not even contact him. In September, Gilman wrote a short email to Martoma to check in on his supposed friend. Martoma remained silent, and the two never spoke again.

The SEC naturally noticed SAC's lucrative trades during the summer of 2008 but could not figure out what had transpired. The breakthrough came in May 2011, when SEC investigators found Martoma's phone number in Gilman's phone records. Ashamed of his actions, Gilman initially lied to the investigators about his communication with Martoma. But Gilman folded when the FBI bluffed that it had recorded the conversations. Gilman's memory of the conversations with Martoma was strangely foggy during the first interview with the SEC and prosecutors. But fog dissipates, and by May 2012, Gilman's recollection of relevant events had improved remarkably, including how he had passed on the content of the PowerPoint slides to Martoma in advance of the infamous Alzheimer's conference. In exchange for his cooperation, Gilman received immunity. He was a small fish in this game, anyway.

Subsequently, the Department of Justice and the SEC used all tools at their disposal to first nail Martoma and then hopefully go up the food chain to nail Steve Cohen. While the evidence against Martoma was compelling, especially Gilman's testimony, Martoma erected an unyielding defense with the financial backing of SAC Capital, pleaded the Fifth, and refused to cooperate. The lack of success in flipping Martoma made it much harder to pursue the case against Cohen.

The SEC and the Department of Justice eventually gathered enough evidence against SAC to take the mammoth hedge fund to court. In late 2013, SAC settled the case, agreeing to stop managing money for outsiders and pay a hefty fine of $1.8 billion. Finally, in 2014, Martoma was found guilty of insider trading and sentenced to nine years of prison and a fine of $9.4 million.

What about Cohen, arguably the main manipulator and beneficiary of the scheme? As many as eight of his former employees were found guilty of insider trading, but Cohen himself got away with a few scratches and a two-year ban from investing funds for outside investors. As if to thumb his nose at government, he paid $155 million dollars for a Picasso painting shortly after the settlement and rebranded SAC Capital as Point72 Asset Management, which would manage his $9 billion fortune.[5] To further his own ego and publicity, he bought the New York Mets in 2020.

Raj Rajaratnam and His South Asian Insider Trading Ring

Raj Rajaratnam grew up in Sri Lanka with a father who worked as the regional head of the Singer Sewing Machine Co. In 1971, ethnic violence in Sri Lanka prompted the family to move to England, where Rajaratnam attended boarding school and studied engineering at the University of Sussex. It was not until he got his MBA from the Wharton School in 1983 that he found his footing in the business world, allowing him to make good use of his charm.[6]

After a short stint at Chase Manhattan Bank, Rajaratnam joined the boutique investment bank Needham & Co in 1985 as an analyst for the computer chip industry. Needham had a reputation for hiring under-dogs and pushing them to their limits. Rajaratnam thrived, working long hours and regularly flying to Palo Alto to talk to executives and dig for information. While his persistence and aggressive tactics frustrated some tech executives, Rajaratnam was so successful that Needham requested that he set up an in-house hedge fund specializing in tech stocks in 1992.

In 1997, Rajaratnam broke away from Needham to start his own hedge fund, Galleon Group, just a block from his old firm. Unlike the frugal culture at Needham, which had limited employees' spending on dinners and travel and even scolded those who discarded redeemable soda cans, the culture at Galleon was flashy and loud; Rajaratnam loved splurging on luxurious parties with "rent-a-dates" and playing periodic oddball pranks. For example, one day he offered his employees $5,000 to be shocked with a stun gun. And as an especially distasteful April Fool's Day gag, he hired a dwarf actor for the day to work as an analyst on "small-cap" stocks.

Rajaratnam continued to work hard at Galleon and expected the same from his employees. Most of the time he spent cultivating sources, extracting information, and searching for potential moles in the industry. He favored targets from the Indian subcontinent, lever-aging their common background. To elevate his standing in the South Asian community, he donated money to various Indian causes, regu-larly attended Indian galas, and raised $7.5 million for victims of the 2004 South Asian tsunami.

With so many moles in Rajaratnam's network, it was inevitable that some would get caught. Many firms grew suspicious of Rajaratnam's tactics and tried to caulk leaks. For example, Intel had long suspected that someone was leaking data to Rajaratnam, so it set up cameras by the fax machine at its headquarters. In 1998, the cameras captured an employee named Roomy Khan sending confidential data on Intel chip orders to Raj. She left Intel soon thereafter and was hired at Galleon.[7]

Perhaps Rajaratnam's biggest scoop was Rajat Gupta. Gupta served the maximum of three three-year terms as the managing director (chief executive) at McKinsey & Co from 1994 to 2003, making him the first Indian to lead a multinational corporation. He was a rock star in the Indian community and served on several high-profile boards, including that of Goldman Sachs from 2006 until his term expired in 2010. Rajaratnam courted Gupta many times over the years. But it was Anil Kumar, one of Rajaratnam's classmates at Wharton and Gupta's protégé, who brought them closer.[8]

Gupta had millions of dollars stowed away from the consulting industry, though nowhere as much as Rajaratnam had made in the hedge fund industry. More importantly, Gupta had a valuable network and stature. In 2006, Rajaratnam and Gupta joined forces to create a new "fund of funds" called Voyager Capital, with Rajaratnam providing the bulk of the seed capital, and most of the fund's money was invested in Galleon. The two developed a complex relationship based on mutual financial interest, and Rajaratnam appeared to have Gupta in a chokehold.

After Gupta joined the Goldman Sachs board in the fall of 2006, Rajaratnam started to squeeze him for information. Gupta delivered under pressure. For example, on March 12, 2007, Gupta dialed into an audit committee meeting from Galleon's offices. The committee previewed Goldman's first-quarter profits, which turned out to be better than expected. Half an hour after Gupta hung up, Galleon bought $91 million of Goldman stock, deviating from its typical concentration in the tech sector and making a quick $2 million.

More famously, at 3:15 p.m. on September 23, 2008, a week after the collapse of Lehman Brothers, Gupta joined a conference call with the Goldman board to approve a $5 billion investment from Warren Buffett. The call lasted less than an hour, and at 3:55 p.m., Gupta called

Rajaratnam. They spoke for only 35 seconds, and a couple of minutes later Rajaratnam bought more than $30 million of Goldman stock.

Rajaratnam became a wealthy man, earning $200 million in 2007 alone. By mid-2008, Galleon had amassed some $8 billion in assets, making it one of the largest hedge funds on Wall Street. But the government was closing in on him.

In 2007, the SEC investigated Rajaratnam's younger brother's hedge fund. Rajaratnam cooperated by answering questions and providing documents, leading the SEC to become suspicious of Galleon. On March 7, 2008, a federal judge gave permission to wiretap Rajaratnam's phone, marking the first time that wiretapping was used to investigate insider trading. Unlike Cohen at SAC Capital, Rajaratnam could be sloppy about how he communicated information. For example, here's what an FBI agent overheard on the evening of July 24, 2008:

Woman: Raj, you better listen to me. Please don't f*ck me on this.

Rajaratnam: Yeah.

Woman: They're gonna guide down. I just got a call from my guy. I played him like a finely tuned piano.

The woman was Danielle Chiesi, a former beauty queen who now lived alone in Midtown and slept with men for stock tips. She used the Wall Street lingo "guide down" to communicate that the earnings of a company called Akamai were lower than investors expected. (Her phone records later revealed that she had talked to a senior executive at Akamai immediately before her conversation with Rajaratnam.) The next day, Rajaratnam placed a bet that Akamai's stock price would fall when it announced its earnings by shorting 138,550 of its shares. The bet paid off; the stock price fell to about $23 upon the earning announcements, down from about $32 when Rajaratnam placed the short, yielding a profit of ($32 − $23) × 138,550 = $1.2 million.

In another wiretap, the SEC overheard Rajaratnam telling a colleague that he had acquired inside information about Goldman's earnings: "I heard yesterday from somebody who's on the board of Goldman Sachs that they are gonna lose $2 per share. The Street has them making $2.50."

The SEC also wiretapped a conversation proving that Rajaratnam had advance information on Warren Buffet's $5 billion investment in Goldman:

Rajaratnam: I got a call at 3:58, right?

Colleague: Yeah.

Rajaratnam: Saying something good might happen to Goldman.

In October 2009, Rajaratnam was arrested for insider trading. He mounted a vigorous fight in court, spending $40 million and arguing that he traded on a mosaic of public information. For example, he paid one million dollars to finance Professor Gregg Jarrell and a research firm Jarrell worked with to develop and present more than three hundred PowerPoint slides filled with stock graphs to prove that Rajaratnam's trades could very well have been based on information in the public domain rather than inside information. But the government had a strong case built on abundant wiretaps and its effective lead witness, Kumar, who cooperated with the prosecutor for leniency.

In October 2011, Rajaratnam was sentenced to eleven years in prison. A year later, in October 2012, Gupta was sentenced to two years in prison. The two met in prison, where they discussed "prison stuff," played *Scrabble* and chess, and ate breakfast together. Gupta continued to maintain his innocence and supposedly forgave Rajaratnam. While Rajaratnam and Gupta were the big fish, they were not the only ones ensnared in the Galleon probe; in total, more than fifty individuals pleaded guilty or were convicted.

In September 2019, two years before his scheduled release, Rajaratnam was released to house arrest. The previous year, President Trump had signed the First Step Act into law (after lobbying by Kim Kardashian) to grant early release to nonviolent criminal offenders over the age of sixty with terminal illness. At age sixty-two and with advanced diabetes, Rajaratnam qualified for such leniency.

The Safe Harbor That Was Not

Given corporate executives' continuous access to inside information, the SEC is particularly suspicious of their trading activities. Executives are even subject to blackout periods around earnings announcements and other major events during which they are not allowed to trade.

To mitigate these suspicions, executives often use prearranged trading plans, committing to future trades in advance. The idea is that any inside information they possess will become public by the time the trades occur, allowing stock prices to adjust accordingly. These plans have generally provided a safe harbor for executives to trade. However, they also present a loophole, as executives can exploit inside information if it's unlikely to become public before the prearranged trades take place.

The first criminal insider trading case based solely on trades placed pursuant to a prearranged trading plan occurred just a few years ago and involved Terren Peizer, the founder and chairman of the healthcare company Ontrak. Interestingly, in the 1980s, Peizer was a protégé of Michael Milken, the notorious junk bond king who pleaded guilty to securities fraud in 1990. Peizer even cooperated in the case against his mentor in exchange for immunity.[9]

In the spring of 2021, Ontrak was struggling. In March 2021, Peizer allegedly learned that Ontrak might lose Cigna as a customer. This would be a major blow, because Cigna contributed more than half of Ontrak's revenues. By the end of April, Cigna had started to scale back its involvement with Ontrak. Recognizing the predicament, Peizer established a prearranged trading plan on May 10 to sell nearly six hundred thousand shares. On the very next day, he started selling, and over the next few months, he sold $19 million worth of Ontrak stock.

On August 13, Peizer established a second plan, under which he started to sell three days later and sold a total of $2 million worth of shares. Then, on August 19, Ontrak announced the loss of a customer with an expected three-year $90 million contract (later revealed to be Cigna), causing the stock to tumble by 45 percent.

Despite claiming not to be part of the information loop, Peizer was convicted in June 2024 of insider trading that circumvented losses of over $12.5 million.

Insider Trading among Members of Congress

Trading on nonpublic information isn't limited to corporate insiders and their collaborators on Wall Street. On November 13, 2011, CBS's *60 Minutes* ran a story called "Congress: Trading Stock on Inside Information." The story alleged that members of Congress routinely exploit nonpublic information and influence for their personal investment decisions. In classic *60 Minutes* style, correspondent Steve Kroft provided several examples of such investments, interviewed experts who scorned the practice, and frantically (but mostly unsuccessfully) sought comments from the culprits.

The first example is particularly egregious. In highly confidential meetings on September 18, 2008, Treasury Secretary Hank Paulson and Federal Reserve Chairman Ben Bernanke informed congressional leaders, including Spencer Bachus, of an impending global financial meltdown. The very next day, Congressman Bachus bought an inverse exchange traded fund (ETF), essentially betting that the economy would collapse.[10] There are two troublesome aspects to this bet. First, it was based on inside information that was not available to the public, including the taxpayers who paid Bachus's $174,000 salary. Second, Bachus now had an incentive to sabotage efforts to revive the economy—not exactly what voters in Alabama had in mind when they elected him.

In most cases, however, members of Congress obtain nonpublic information that pertains to narrower segments of the economy. For instance, in 2009, House Minority Leader John Boehner led the opposition against government-funded health insurance while simultaneously trading health insurance stocks in his personal portfolio. In this case, it's likely that Boehner had access to nonpublic information about health insurance companies that could affect their stock values. Even more disturbing, Boehner was likely in a position to influence the value of health insurance stocks through his actions. If so, his trading in health insurance stocks created a conflict of interest, because he would be inclined to take actions that benefited his portfolio rather than the country he had pledged to serve.

Other members of Congress used their power more explicitly for personal financial gains. In 2005, Speaker of the House Dennis Hastert helped earmark $207 million to build the Prairie Parkway near his Illinois home. But before that, he had strategically bought some adjacent land, which he sold at a $2 million profit five months after the earmarking. Similarly, Senator Judd Gregg of New Hampshire helped steer $70 million toward redeveloping a defunct Air Force base in which he had a commercial interest. And House Speaker Nancy Pelosi might have exploited her influence when she purchased shares in Visa's IPO while credit card legislation made its way through the House.

The *60 Minutes* story gave rise to a public outcry that members of Congress undoubtedly heard loud and clear. Notably, seven years earlier, legislation had been proposed to make it illegal for members of Congress to trade on nonpublic information. Despite its clever acronym, the Stop Trading on Congressional Knowledge (STOCK) Act received minimal support. If anything, the need for such legislation had only grown stronger since then, with a rapidly expanding political intelligence industry of former congress members and staffers scouring the hallways of Capitol Hill in search of information they could sell to hedge funds and other investors.

With enough political momentum and bipartisan support, Congress can move quickly. Less than five months after the *60 Minutes* story aired, President Barack Obama signed the STOCK Act into law to much fanfare on April 4, 2012. Among other things, the act prohibits members of Congress, the executive branch, and their staffs from using nonpublic information for personal gain and requires securities transactions in excess of $1,000 to be filed within forty-five days.[11] However, the penalty for late filing is small—only $200 for the first offense—and is often ignored or waived by House or Senate ethics officials.

As of 2025, no member of Congress had been charged under the STOCK Act. This doesn't mean that there haven't been controversial trades but rather that Congress, as the first line of defense in enforcing the act, has been reluctant to investigate its own members, and the burden of proof for insider trading under the act is high. Perhaps the most controversial trades occurred as the COVID-19 virus was spreading at the beginning of 2020. At that time, Senator Richard Burr, one of just three senators who had opposed the STOCK Act several years earlier, was the chairman of the Senate Intelligence Committee and had a unique perspective on the threat of the outbreak and the government's response.

In a coauthored op-ed dated February 7, 2020, Burr wrote that "the United States today is better prepared than ever before to face emerging public health threats, like the coronavirus." In a press release dated March 5, 2020, he echoed his sentiment: "Luckily, we have a framework in place that has put us in a better position than any other country to respond to a public health threat, like the coronavirus." However, National Public Radio (NPR) obtained a secret recording from an exclusive luncheon on February 27, 2020, in which Burr warned attendees that the virus "is much more aggressive in its transmission than anything that we have seen in recent history" and that schools could close and the military be mobilized.

Furthermore, on February 13, Burr sold stock worth about $1 million, including $250,000 of hotel stocks. Such a large sale was highly unusual for Burr and helped him dodge hundreds of thousands of dollars in losses as the virus outbreak took a toll on the economy and the stock market. Burr insisted he had traded on public information yet preemptively stepped down from the Intelligence Committee. After a long investigation, the Justice Department stated on January 19, 2021, that it would not pursue insider trading charges. Two years after, the SEC announced that it closed its probe into the matter with no enforcement action.

The Large Sample Evidence on Illegal Insider Trading

Uncovering trading on inside information is tricky for a couple of reasons. First, examining the public record of corporate insiders' trades is often futile. The SEC mandates corporate insiders to report trades in their own companies in a timely manner. When they comply, we can readily examine the trades to see if they coincide with major news announcements and movements in stock prices. However, corporate insiders realize that their reported trades are scrutinized. Therefore, they are wary of reporting trades that are based on material nonpublic information.

Second, the severe insider trading probably occurs in dark alleys of Wall Street, where connections between trades and the source of the inside information are obscured. Consider the case of Mathew Martoma. While the SEC could see that SAC Capital made some exceptionally profitable trades around Elan and Wyeth's major stock price movements, it was very hard to identify how SAC Capital might have gained inside information. The SEC had to examine all kinds of possible connections between SAC Capital traders and insiders at Elan and Wyeth, and it lucked out when it discovered records of telephone calls between Martoma and Sid Gilman, who wasn't even a true insider. The SEC was also fortunate in that Gilman cooperated, as the evidence would otherwise have been too circumstantial to secure a conviction. In other cases, the culprits might be more careful not to leave behind evidence of communication that survives over time, or they might not be so easily swayed to cooperate with investigators.

Consequently, we're up against some major barriers when trying to document aggregate patterns of insider trading. Yet some researchers have made headway.

In a study published in the *Journal of Finance* in 2012, Lauren Cohen, Christopher Malloy, and Lukasz Pomorski examined reported corporate insider trading records. Because these trades are regulated and scrutinized, most are not based on material inside information. As a first step, the researchers therefore aimed to weed out trades that were highly unlikely to be based on inside information. Specifically, they identified what they called *routine trades*, which occur at regular intervals. These include purchases of stock when insiders receive bonuses or when their executive stock options vest, or sales of stock on a predetermined schedule to avoid allegations of insider trading. After removing the routine trades, the researchers were left with a sample of trades they called *opportunistic trades*, which are *more* likely (though not necessarily very likely) to be based on inside information. In the second step, the researchers estimated the stock returns during the month after the trades. They also partitioned the returns into the *normal* and *abnormal* portions, where the normal portion is the return for benchmark stocks with similar risk profiles during the same period, and the abnormal portion is simply the remainder of the return.

A drumroll, please, for the main results: opportunistic stock purchases are associated with an average stock return of 2.3 percent during the following month, which appears to be about 1.5 percent more than what is normal. In other words, these stock purchases appear to be particularly well timed, which the authors attribute to insiders' exploitation of nonpublic information.

Opportunistic stock sales are associated with an average stock return of 0.8 percent during the following month, which appears to be about 0.2 percent *below* what is normal. Thus, there's very modest evidence that these stock sales are based on nonpublic information.

In short, Cohen et al. provided convincing evidence that corporate insiders base some of their nonroutine purchases of stock on nonpublic information. However, the return figures are modest, so the ill-gotten gains from the nonroutine purchases seem small. Presumably, if they wished to make larger profits from their inside information, they would secretly pass the information to investors who don't have to file their trades or are at least an arm's length away from the insiders.

Yes, I know this is a bit of a letdown, especially when the results were preceded by a drumroll. So far, we haven't been able to uncover massive insider trading. Let's move on to another study, this one related to the growing political intelligence industry mentioned earlier.

In their 2020 study published in the *Journal of Finance*, Alan Jagolinzer, David Larcker, Gaizka Ormazabal, and Daniel Taylor examined whether corporate insiders (yes, corporate insiders, not politicians) might use nonpublic information from the political arena in their stock trading. More specifically, they examined whether executives and directors at banks traded on confidential information about the government bailout program during the financial crisis of 2007 to 2008.

Let's take a step back first. During the financial crisis, government officials met privately with executives at leading financial institutions to deliberate the government intervention, including the terms of the giant Troubled Asset Relief Program (TARP). The allocation of the hundreds of billions of dollars of TARP money would have large effects on financial institutions, including their stock prices. Therefore, anybody with access to the private deliberations would gain an informational advantage that could be exploited in the stock market.

The researchers first identified corporate insiders who were most likely to have access to the private deliberations through their professional network. To do that, they classified insiders at 497 banks as politically connected if any of the bank's board members had previous work experience at the Federal Reserve, Treasury, a bank regulator, or Congress. Then the researchers partitioned their sample period from July 2005 to June 2011 into four periods: (1) the two-year precrisis period, (2) the financial crisis period before the bailout in October 2008, (3) the financial crisis period after the bailout, and (4) the two-year postcrisis period. Figure 6-2 shows the level of the S&P 500 for each of these periods, along with the perfect timing of the Bachus trade discussed earlier. Finally, the researchers

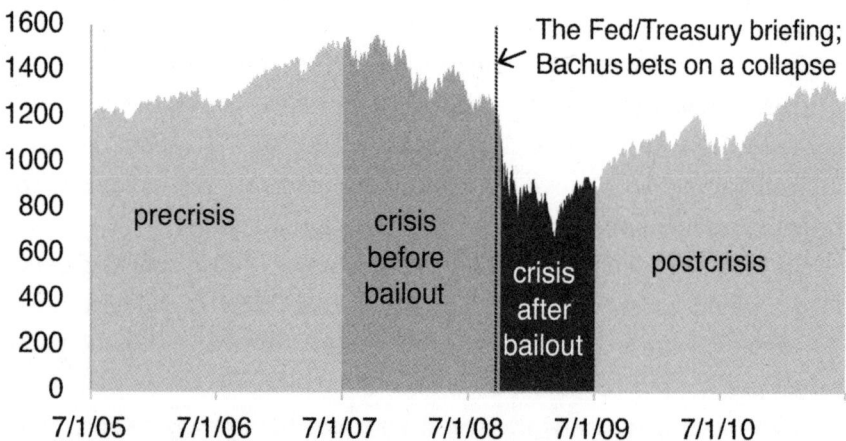

Figure 6-2. Performance of the S&P 500 during four subperiods around the financial crisis.

estimated the stock returns after the trades made by the politically connected corporate insiders during each of the four periods.

As the researchers had predicted, they really didn't find much of
interest during the first two periods. But they found some disturbing
results for the crisis period after the bailout. Specifically, during this
period, the politically connected insiders apparently made very advan-
tageous trades:

- Following their stock purchases, the average monthly return was
  5 percent, yielding a healthy profit.

- Following their stock sales, the average monthly return was –4 percent, meaning they avoided substantial losses.

This evidence suggests that politically connected insiders had an
informational advantage that they traded on during the crisis, especially
during the period when the TARP money flowed through the economy.
As the financial crisis ended, the value of bank insiders' political connections dwindled.[12]

Although these academic studies were cleverly designed, neither
captures the egregious examples of insider trading described earlier;
they barely scratched the surface. Perhaps no study will effectively cap-
ture the trading on inside information throughout Wall Street, meaning
we'll never have an accurate estimate of how much profit is made from
illegal insider trading. This is the kind of challenge that keeps researchers up at night, and now it might keep you up too.

7

Banking's Biggest Bluff:
The LIBOR Manipulation

Give a man a gun and he can rob a bank.
Give a man a bank and he can rob the world.

—TYRELL WELLICK, *Mr. Robot*

Every morning, in the heart of London, a number was calculated that would influence trillions of dollars of financial transactions around the globe. This was LIBOR (the London Interbank Offered Rate), the interest rate that banks claimed they would charge each other for loans. It served as the benchmark for everything from ordinary mortgages to complex derivatives and massive corporate deals.

But behind the scenes, a cabal of insiders conspired to rig this rate, distorting the very foundation of the financial markets. Traders aimed to move decimal points to favor their trading positions, while bankers did their best not to stick out with a high borrowing rate, behaving like a coordinated herd of sheep (see Figure 7-1).

This chapter uncovers the mechanisms of the fraud, the key players involved, and the far-reaching consequences of their actions. The colossal scandal makes Bernie Madoff look like a street-corner three-card monte hustler.

Figure 7-1. Bankers as a herd of sheep.

The World's Most Important Number and Other Interest Rates

While it's a bit technical, we should start with a broad overview of key interest rates in the capital market arena. First, the *Treasury yield* is the interest rate that the US government pays on its debt obligations. This rate varies depending on the maturity of the debt, with longer maturities typically having higher yields, and it is influenced by general market conditions. The Treasury yield is widely regarded as a risk-free rate because it is highly unlikely that the US government will default on its scheduled debt payments. We'll leverage this risk-free attribute later.

Another important rate is the *Fed funds rate*, which is the average rate at which US banks lend each other funds in the overnight market. US banks are required to keep a reserve equal to a fraction (usually 10 percent) of their deposits at a Federal Reserve bank. Any funds that exceed this requirement can be lent to banks with shortfalls. While the Fed funds rate is negotiated among the banks and essentially determined by demand and supply for funds, the Federal Open Market Committee (FOMC) of the Federal Reserve System sets a *target rate* for the Fed funds rate at its eight annual meetings. This target rate is the one we hear about on the news and that can shake up the financial markets when it changes unexpectedly. Once the FOMC has set the target, the Federal Reserve uses open market operations, like buying or selling government bonds (essentially tinkering with demand and supply for funds), to steer the Fed funds rate toward the target. Despite the media attention on the Fed funds rate, I will leave it aside for the rest of this chapter.

Finally, we get to LIBOR, often referred to as "the world's most important number." LIBOR was supposed to be the average of the interest rates at which a panel of about sixteen leading international banks could borrow from other banks. Every trading day around 11:00 a.m. GMT, designated individuals at banks on the LIBOR panel would submit their estimates of what it would have cost them to borrow at that precise time. The estimates were almost always based on hypothetical scenarios rather than real transactions, relying on an honor system. Yes, you read that correctly—the LIBOR system relied on bankers acting honorably! This inherent weakness is significant, and we'll return to it.

Thomson Reuters would receive the estimates from the panel banks, calculate the average based on the two middle quartiles, and announce the official LIBOR around 11:30 a.m. In addition, the submissions by individual panel banks were released. By excluding outliers from the calculation, LIBOR was thought to be less susceptible, though not immune, to errors and manipulation. This process was replicated across about ten of the main currencies and more than ten maturities ranging from one day to a year to form more than a hundred different LIBORs. For simplicity, I will mostly refer to LIBOR as if it were a single rate.

Figure 7-2 provides the sixteen submissions for the three-month US dollar LIBOR between 11:00 and 11:10 a.m. GMT on April 15, 2008.[1] They range from 2.70 percent for Citigroup and Deutsche Bank, to 2.75 percent for Halifax Bank of Scotland (HBOS). The average of the two middle quartiles of 2.71594 percent was published at 11:30 GMT.

Why would the submitted rates differ across banks? The most obvious explanation is the difference in credit risk, with Citigroup and Deutsche Bank being financially stronger than the others, as

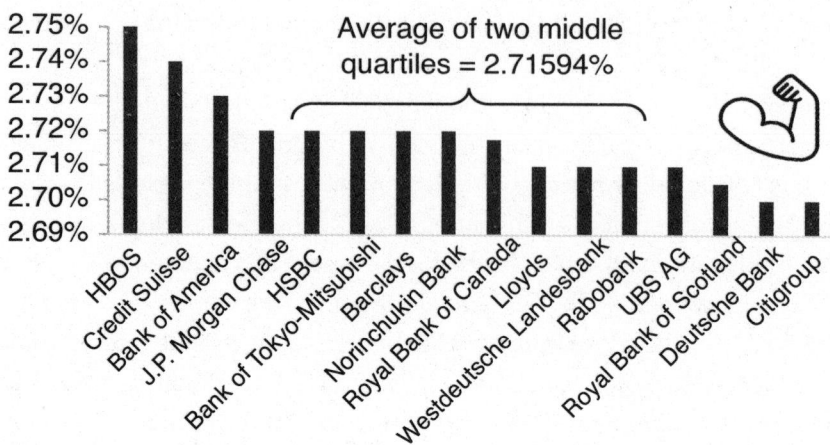

Figure 7-2. LIBOR submissions on April 15, 2008.

indicated by the picture of the flexing muscle in the figure. To be a bit technical, the variation in rates due to credit risk is known as the *credit spread*. That means that we can view LIBOR as the sum of the risk-free rate—the rate that investors view to be guaranteed—and the average credit spread of the submitters (or at least the average for the banks whose submissions ended up being used to estimate the LIBOR). Also, recall that the Treasury yield is a common proxy for the risk-free rate, meaning that LIBOR should be the sum of the Treasury yield and the average credit spread.

At this point, you might be wondering where I'm going with this. Be patient, and you'll see. The insight that LIBOR should be the sum of the Treasury yield and the credit spread, or alternatively, that the credit spread should equal LIBOR minus the Treasury yield, will be crucial in proving manipulation.

Figure 7-3 shows the three-month Treasury yield, the three-month US dollar LIBOR rate, and the credit spread (estimated as the difference between the Treasury yield and LIBOR) at monthly intervals from 2002 to 2020. Between 2002 and 2007, the credit spread was consistently below 1 percent. When the financial crisis hit, the difference spiked, peaking in October 2008 above 3 percent, just a few weeks after Lehman Brothers filed for bankruptcy on September 15, 2008.[2] The spike made perfect sense; with several financial institutions folding and others rumored to be in trouble, the capital market increased its estimated probability that the panel of banks would struggle to pay their debt.

It's time to unveil the first sign of deceit. This sign is based on suspicious clustering of observations in the distribution. (As a teaser, the evidence that follows in a later section is based on some clever benchmarking instead.)

If you examine the LIBOR during the year leading up to the financial crisis, you'll notice it remained suspiciously stable, even as the Treasury yield fluctuated. You might need to pull out the magnifying glass from your detective set to see it clearly. Let me provide a compelling statistic based on daily data: out of more than four thousand three-month LIBOR submissions from August 2006 through July 2007, a staggering 40 percent were exactly 5.36 percent, with another 20 percent at either 5.35 percent or 5.37 percent. The clustering of observations was even more pronounced for one-month LIBOR submissions, with 67 percent at exactly 5.32 percent. Clearly, something was amiss.

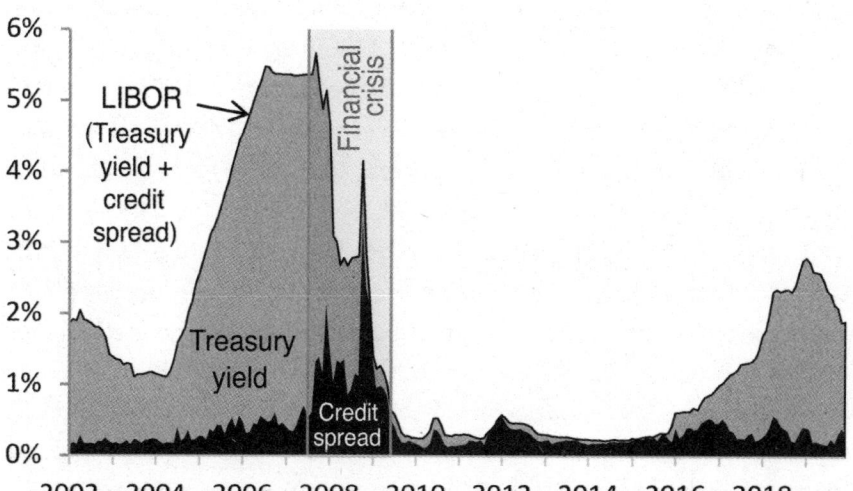

Figure 7-3. LIBOR, Treasury yield, and credit spread.

Riding Their Own Waves

We've just observed that the credit spread for the panel of LIBOR banks remained consistently below 1 percent from 2002 to 2020, except during the two years surrounding the financial crisis, when it surged. During the crisis, it was crucial for banks to project strength to maintain confidence among customers and investors.

One way for banks to demonstrate financial strength is by reporting a low borrowing rate. But what if the actual borrowing rate isn't that low? Well, maybe they can pretend that it is. This is where the reporting system for the LIBOR calculation comes into play. Remember that the panel banks submit the borrowing rates that they would have paid if they had borrowed from another bank that same morning. Of course, most banks do not actually borrow on a given morning, effectively giving them some flexibility in the rates they submit. The lax oversight accentuates this flexibility.

In the earlier LIBOR calculation example, suppose that HBOS wanted to display strength by submitting a borrowing rate in line with the stronger banks. Specifically, instead of submitting a rate of 2.75 percent, say HBOS submitted a lowball rate of 2.71 percent, making it look like it was among the stronger banks in the panel rather than the weakest. As a result of this hypothetical manipulation, LIBOR would drop very slightly from 2.71594 percent to 2.71469 percent, a reduction of 0.00125 percent. Also, the standard deviation (a measure of variation) across all submissions would decrease from 0.0135 percent to 0.0105 percent, indicating that the submissions are more clustered.

In this example, HBOS's goal was not to manipulate LIBOR but to submit a rate that showed strength. In other words, the LIBOR effect was unintentional. It is easy to imagine that if one bank lowballs its estimate, other banks follow suit, both because banks look at other submitted rates for guidance and because no bank wants to stand out with a high rate. The result could be a cascade of downward manipulations, which, in turn, would have a significant downward effect on LIBOR.

Alternatively, some banks might manipulate their submitted rates with the deliberate goal of affecting LIBOR, sometimes upward and other times downward. But to better understand this, we first need to understand how LIBOR was used.

LIBOR used to be a common benchmark rate throughout the financial world. Financial institutions used LIBOR as a reference for setting interest rates on various debt instruments, including government bonds, corporate bonds, and mortgages. For example, a company might issue bonds with a floating interest rate equal to the prevailing LIBOR plus a spread of 2 percent, meaning that a LIBOR of 3.5 percent would imply interest of 3.5 percent + 2 percent = 5.5 percent. Naturally, an increase in LIBOR would raise interest payments, and vice versa. Additionally, a major portion of derivatives like futures and swaps too complex to discuss here were linked to LIBOR. In total, more than $300 *trillion* in financial products was pegged to LIBOR. In comparison, the gross domestic product (GDP) for the entire world was a little more than $100 trillion in 2024. Thus, even tiny changes in LIBOR could trigger giant transfers of wealth.

With so much value at stake, many players in the financial market would love to have a say in the setting of LIBOR. This was not a poker game in some dark basement. The individual actions sent ripple effects throughout the financial system, like a pebble thrown into a pond, creating waves that spread far and wide.[3]

The question then arises: Could traders who stood to benefit from changes in LIBOR influence the submissions of the panel banks? For at least a few of them, the answer is yes. In fact, some traders were submitters themselves, while others worked for banks on the LIBOR panel where the submitters had standing orders to assist their colleagues. Moreover, in our corrupt world, influence can be bought, sometimes surprisingly cheaply, such as with a bottle of good whiskey.

More Tracks Left by the Herd

In November 2007, just a few months into the financial crisis and with the credit spread for the panel of LIBOR banks nearing 2 percent, the

Bank of England hosted a meeting for a group of British bankers. By the end of that meeting, suspicions had taken root that panel banks were lowballing their submission rates. The minutes from the meeting stated that "several group members thought that Libor fixings had been lower than actual traded interbank rates through the period of stress." These concerns were echoed in the minutes from a Bank of England meeting on April 3, 2008: "U.S. dollar Libor rates had at times appeared lower than actual traded interbank rates."

Concerns also surfaced on the other side of the Atlantic. On April 10, Citigroup issued a five-page report to its clients and a handful of reporters titled "Is LIBOR Broken?" Written by Citigroup analyst Scott Peng, the report suggested that LIBOR was understated by twenty to thirty basis points. The following day, April 11, 2008, an unnamed Barclays tipster called Fabiola Ravazzolo of the New York Fed and professed that Barclays deliberately underreported its rates: "We know that we are not posting, um, an honest LIBOR. . . . We are doing it, because, um, if we didn't do it, it draws, um, unwanted attention on ourselves."

Carrick Mollenkamp, working for the *Wall Street Journal*'s London office, picked up the chatter among the bankers and quickly gathered that it was an open secret that LIBOR was rigged. By the time he received Peng's report, he was already working on his own article, "Libor Fog: Bankers Cast Doubt on Key Rate Amid Crisis," published in the *Wall Street Journal* on April 16, 2008. Mollenkamp argued that "some banks don't want to report the high rates they're paying for short-term loans because they don't want to tip off the market that they're desperate for cash." Building on this argument, he relayed the concerns in the banking community "about whether banks are reporting rates that reflect their true borrowing costs."

While Mollenkamp was unable to find anyone to speak on record about LIBOR manipulation, he mentioned a recent incident in which banks had paid 0.1 percent more when they borrowed from the Federal Reserve than they would have paid had they borrowed from peer banks as per LIBOR, even though Fed loans require securities as collateral and are therefore safer. Why wouldn't the banks rather borrow at the lower rate and avoid putting up collateral? This indicated that LIBOR should have been at the very least 0.1 percent higher.

Mollenkamp had clearly struck a nerve in the banking community. The chatter intensified, and the submitters appear to have been temporarily spooked. Figure 7-4 shows the daily standard deviation of the submission rates in the month before and after the *Wall Street Journal* article was published. The standard deviation measures the dispersion of submissions for the various banks. A low standard deviation indicates clustering of submissions, as would be the case if the submitters were just following each other like sheep in a herd. The standard deviation surged the day after publication, and it took a few weeks for it to come down to prepublication levels. Thus, it seems the article startled the herd for a while. However, the credit spread, based on the difference between LIBOR and the Treasury yield, stayed constant in the days around the publication and actually decreased slowly in the weeks afterward. This suggests that submitters did not back off their efforts to show strength by submitting a low LIBOR relative to the Treasury yield; their efforts were just less coordinated.[4]

Mollenkamp was not finished by a long shot. Together with his editor, Mark Whitehouse, he followed up with another influential article,

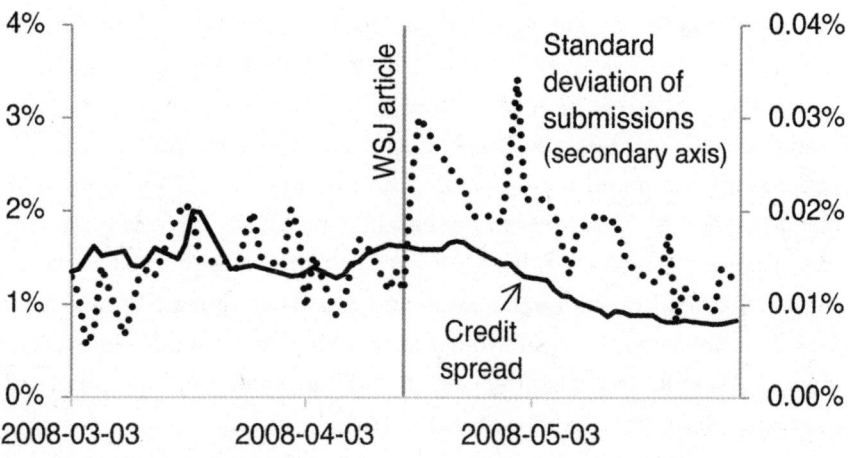

Figure 7-4. Credit spread and the standard deviation of LIBOR submissions.

"Study Casts Doubt on Key Rate," published in the *Wall Street Journal* on May 29, 2008. By then, the two London-based journalists had gathered much more data and consulted with three academics with expertise in finance and statistics to *prove* that LIBOR was manipulated. In short, they came ready to fight.

For each bank in the LIBOR panel, Mollenkamp and Whitehouse had collected the submitted rates and subtracted the Treasury yield to get the credit spreads from the end of January to the middle of April. Then they posed the question: Were the submitted rates, and by extension, the credit spreads, artificially low? To answer this question, Mollenkamp and Whitehouse needed a benchmark for what the credit spreads should have been for the panel banks in the absence of manipulation.

It turns out that the credit spread is readily available for individual bond issues in the credit default swap (CDS) market. *CDSs*, which gained notoriety during the financial crisis because many experts blamed them for fueling it, are essentially insurance contracts that investors can buy to hedge against bond defaults.[5] Thus, the combination of a bond and a CDS is the same as a risk-free bond, like a Treasury bond. Brilliant insight, right? This further implies that the *CDS spread*, meaning the annual cost of the CDS as a fraction of the principal value of the bond, should equal the bond's credit spread. If a bank's CDS spread exceeds its credit spread based on its submission toward LIBOR, one might conclude that the submitted rate was too low, and perhaps even intentionally so.

When Mollenkamp and Whitehouse compared their estimated credit spreads for the panel banks based on submitted rates to the CDS spreads for the panel banks' outstanding bonds, they found conspicuous gaps. None of the sixteen panel banks had CDS spreads below the credit spread based on LIBOR submissions on average. For Citigroup, the CDS spread on its bonds exceeded the credit spread based on its LIBOR submissions by more than 0.8 percent on average! The average gaps for Westdeutsche Landesbank and HBOS were not that far behind, at roughly 0.7 percent and 0.6 percent, respectively.[6]

This was an impressive piece of journalism, going far beyond what is typically taught in journalism school. One could argue that it met academia's rigorous standards for novelty and quality and could have been published in a respectable academic journal. It also shows the societal value of having investigative journalists with both time and resources to dig deep.

Despite the compelling evidence of banks lowballing their LIBOR submissions, Mollenkamp and Whitehouse were careful in their allegations. They even included a couple of caveats in their analysis, noting that estimates of borrowing rates involve a lot of guesswork and that the market for CDSs is volatile, and was especially so during the financial crisis. These data issues could explain why the CDS spread would occasionally exceed the credit spread from LIBOR submissions, but not why it was consistently higher for several months for several of the panel banks. The collective power of the large number of observations was simply too strong for the results to be coincidental.

After the *Wall Street Journal* published Mollenkamp and Whitehouse's analysis, several researchers from academia conducted independent analyses using even more data and alternative methods. The general conclusions held up: the LIBOR submissions were too low and too clustered during the financial crisis to not have been rigged. It appeared as if the bankers behaved like sheep, where no one wanted their submission to stick out, especially on the high side.

You might have noticed that the evidence primarily pertains to banks lowballing submissions and staying within the range of their competitors. There is no good study showing the extent of LIBOR manipulation for the purpose of boosting trading profits. However, we have some insight from the culprits themselves, which brings us to the next section.

It Takes a Village

How did the manipulation occur? The LIBOR manipulations culminated in numerous investigations, court cases (with accompanying discovery processes), and journalistic inquiries, all of which uncovered many backstories, especially about manipulation intended to boost trading profits. The wealth of information resulted in three books about the scandal, with *The Spider Network* by David Enrich, published in 2017, being the best known. A *Wall Street Journal* journalist at the time, Enrich gained unique access to key players in the scandal, allowing him to write a thrilling account of the events. It became clear that the manipulation was spread across a wide network of traders and brokers, with one of the hubs being Tom Hayes, the main character in Enrich's book. Here's a brief synopsis, with a focus on how traders manipulated LIBOR for trading gains.

It's uncertain how and where the manipulation all started. Submitting rates for the LIBOR calculations was viewed as an administrative task for junior employees. Some of these employees sought input from traders within the bank, while others simply submitted what they learned from informal conversations that other banks would submit. Gradually, traders and bank executives must have understood the weakness of this system and the ease with which LIBOR could be manipulated. Those with the most to gain from LIBOR movements and the least integrity must have encouraged the submitters to nudge the LIBOR in a favorable direction. The manipulation likely began independently in several banks and flourished well before the turn of the century.

When Tom Hayes entered the investment banking business in 2001, it was already common knowledge in pockets of the banking community that LIBOR was being manipulated. Hayes was not a stereotypical trader, if one exists. He was more of a mathematician—brilliant with numbers and socially awkward, even avoiding eye contact when talking to others. He dressed casually and preferred to eat comfort food while watching TV to eating at fancy restaurants and drinking at hip bars. Superstitious by nature, he often wore lucky socks and a T-shirt with the logo of his favorite soccer team, Queens Park Rangers, which ironically read "Destined for Glory." Behind his back, his colleagues called him *Rain Man* (from the Dustin Hoffman movie), and he was later diagnosed with Asperger's syndrome.

Hayes started his trading career at Royal Bank of Scotland, working on a team that specialized in financial securities derived from Japanese interest rates. In 2002, he became responsible for a small portion of the team's trading. To execute trades, he used several brokers, including Terry Farr at RP Martin and Darrell Read at ICAP. Hayes quickly recognized the value of these brokers, not only for anonymously implementing his trades, but also as a source of information and later as a conduit for influencing LIBOR. As Hayes's trading and brokerage commissions increased, so did the brokers' desire to please him.

Hayes proved to be a gifted trader. His knack for numbers and lack of social life made him adept at scouring research reports and data in search of profitable trading strategies. Nevertheless, in 2004, he suffered losses on instruments he wasn't authorized to trade, forcing him to resign. Luckily, he already had an offer from the Royal Bank of Canada (RBC), which he accepted, leaving his record unblemished.

Hayes found great success at RBC. In the spring of 2006, the Bank of Japan raised interest rates to 0.25 percent, stirring some volatility in Japanese-linked securities. Hayes was perfectly positioned for this, and by early summer, he was making millions for RBC. That same summer, UBS recruited Hayes to work in its Tokyo office with prospects of more money and prestige.

In his role trading derivatives linked to Japanese interest rates, the yen LIBOR was crucial, and so were related interest rates like TIBOR (*Tokyo* Interbank Offered Rate). At UBS, the person responsible for submitting rates for TIBOR sat next to the traders, and collaboration between submitters and traders had been ongoing long before Hayes had arrived. Hayes recognized the behavior from his time at RBC and wanted to get into the game himself. Unfortunately, LIBOR submitters at UBS were spread across cities worldwide, but not in Tokyo. So, if Hayes wanted to nudge LIBOR, he would have to reach out beyond UBS's Tokyo office.

Roger Darin, the trader at UBS's Singapore office who submitted the yen LIBOR, was initially happy to help Hayes. Like many submitters, Darin had marching orders to assist the firm's traders as much as possible. However, once Hayes encroached on Darin's territory, Darin's attitude changed, compelling Hayes to seek help outside UBS.

Colin Goodman, a.k.a. Lord LIBOR, was the yen LIBOR submitter at ICAP. Every trading day, he sent out an email called "SUGGESTED

LIBORS" to individuals both inside and outside ICAP. These emails were considered a valuable service to ICAP clients, but other LIBOR submitters also received them. Incompetent or lazy submitters, or those who wanted to make sure not to deviate from other submissions, would simply submit the rates from the email. In one email, one of the suggested rates contained a nontrivial typo, yet the rate was still submitted by a couple of banks, showing their inattention and lax attitude toward the process.

Via his ICAP broker, Darrell Read, Hayes connected with Goodman. Hayes regularly asked Goodman to alter the rates in his daily email to move LIBOR in the direction that favored Hayes's positions. For instance, in an email on March 23, 2007, Hayes stated that he "really need[s] a high/unchanged 1m LIBOR today," and Goodman complied. This was highly valuable to Hayes. In one instance, he informed Read that he stood to gain or lose "about 3m usd a bp," meaning that a 0.01 percent change in LIBOR would trigger a $3 million change in the value of his position.

In return, Goodman received kickbacks from UBS. Over time, he negotiated a regular bonus for his LIBOR efforts, and UBS paid ICAP a monthly fee for his services. The financial world, after all, operates on the concept of quid pro quo. Hayes also regularly paid his brokers bonuses under the table with so-called wash trades, in which Hayes would buy and sell the same security in rapid succession just to generate fees for the brokers.

Hayes became obsessed with manipulating LIBOR. He actively used his network of brokers and traders to exert influence and expanded his network when needed. For example, Terry Farr's colleague at RP Martin, Jim Gilmour, had a good relationship with Rabobank's LIBOR submitter, Paul "Pooks" Robson, who at some point slashed his submission from 0.71 to 0.63 for Hayes.

Despite his determination, Hayes was not always able to sway people to help him move LIBOR. His brash behavior and financial success had earned him many enemies, though he was not necessarily aware of this. In the financial world, it's often difficult to distinguish friends from foes, and this was even more challenging for someone with Asperger's. When

Hayes resigned from UBS for a more lucrative position at Citigroup in 2009, he left behind several individuals who felt betrayed by him. These individuals not only were unwilling to help Hayes afterward, but also traded against his positions to inflict losses.

At Citigroup, Hayes encountered more resistance than he had at UBS. Many people at Citigroup simply did not like the arrogant new-comer who had been hired with a $3 million signing bonus. Additionally, Citigroup's submitter was under strict orders to keep Citigroup's sub-missions in line with those of its competitors. Finally, Citigroup felt the pressure from emerging investigations into LIBOR submissions to main-tain a clean record. When Hayes continued to pester his colleagues at Citigroup for assistance with LIBOR, someone alerted the compliance office. This triggered an internal investigation, which concluded that Hayes had attempted to manipulate LIBOR and TIBOR and had failed to fully cooperate with the investigators. Hayes was promptly fired, mark-ing the end of his career in the investment banking world.

Hayes was arrested in December 2012 and received a fourteen-year prison sentence in August 2015, among the longest for a white-collar crime in Britain. While in prison, Hayes became a Christian, and he was released in January 2021.

Paying the Price

As the scandal unfolded, banks and higher-ups tried to distance them-selves by blaming the behavior on a few rogue traders rather than a system failure. However, they couldn't avoid fines totaling roughly $10 billion and significant resignations. Here are a few notable examples:

- In June 2012, Barclays was fined $450 million. A few days later, Marcus Agius resigned as chairman and Bob Diamond as CEO.

- In December 2012, UBS was fined more than $1.7 billion. Inves-tigations revealed that UBS traders had colluded with traders at other panel banks and had made more than two thousand written requests for movements in rates from 2005 to 2010.

- In October 2013, Rabobank was fined more than €700 million.

- In December 2013, Royal Bank of Scotland was fined $1.1 billion and Société Générale was fined $600 million.

- In April 2015, Deutsche Bank was fined $2.5 billion.

Several changes were made to the LIBOR process to make it less vulnerable to manipulation. The push to discard LIBOR began around the same time. In 2023, the massive effort to replace LIBOR with the Secured Overnight Financing Rate (SOFR) was completed in the United States. SOFR is based on actual transactions in the overnight repo market, where large financial institutions enter repurchase agreements (repos) to buy and sell Treasury securities one day and reverse the transactions the following day at slightly higher prices. These repos effectively serve as overnight loans with Treasury securities as collateral, and the price increases reflect the borrowing rates.

In the aftermath of the LIBOR scandal, the financial world was left reeling from the revelation that its most trusted benchmark had been compromised. Should we be surprised that the honor system was abused? What is truly astonishing is how long the deceptive practices persisted, despite being widely suspected. This reveals a deeper truth about financial markets: sometimes the most damaging frauds are the ones hiding in plain sight.

8

Hindsight Is 20/20:
The Stock Option
Backdating Saga

Backdating is bad for America.

—PRESIDENT GEORGE W. BUSH

Imagine if time were not a linear path but a tool to be manipulated. This surreal premise sets the stage for perhaps the most widespread fraud ever in corporate America, where executives and board members discovered how to quietly tap companies for billions of dollars over more than a decade.

Backdating stock options is the financial equivalent of a magician's trick, where the illusion of time is bent to create the perfect moment for profit. Executives, with a wink and a nod, reach back into the past to cherry-pick a date when stock prices hit rock bottom, as shown in Figure 8-1, granting themselves options that are already "in the money." It's a move that can turn a modest compensation package into a windfall, all while leaving unsuspecting shareholders in the dark.

The widespread practice was not well known to outsiders until the *Wall Street Journal* published a series of exposés in 2006, which led to what *BusinessWeek* called "the biggest corporate probe since the mid-1970s" involving federal investigators, the SEC, the US Senate, and

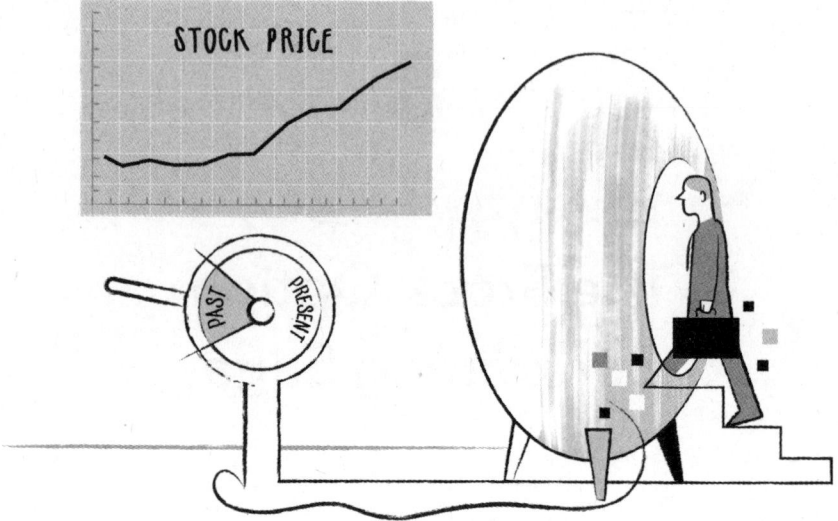

Figure 8-1. Stepping back in time to set the terms of option grants.

plaintiff lawyers. The culpable companies did their best to keep a low profile and quietly entered legal settlements. But at least seventy top officials lost their jobs, and some went to prison. Even Steve Jobs got entangled in the scandal but managed to extricate himself out of trouble by sacrificing a couple of subordinates.

What was all the fuss about? Let's proceed slowly with the basics of executive compensation and option grants.

Stock Options as Compensation

Top executives of US corporations are very well compensated. The average annual CEO compensation among S&P 500 companies is close to $20 million, a few hundred times more than that of typical workers. While a portion of executive compensation comes in the form of regular salary, a much larger portion comes from bonuses, stock, and stock options, all of which can be manipulated in various ways.

But what exactly are these stock options that the executives receive? Executives are granted *call options* on the stock of the firm they work for, which allow the executives to buy stock in their firm at a fixed price, known as the *exercise price*, within a specified period.[1] Just like regular stocks, call options increase in value with the stock price. Moreover, to the extent that the executives' performance affects the stock price, call options increase in value with managerial performance. Therefore, call options can be used as a tool to incentivize executives to perform well, and grants of call options to executives are categorized as "performance-based compensation."

The popularity of executive stock option grants can be attributed to several factors. First, as just mentioned, stock options serve as an incentive for executives to perform and take actions that boost the stock price, thereby aligning their interests with those of shareholders. Second, tax rules favor the use of options. In the early 1990s, politicians were outraged by excessive executive compensation, especially because it was subsidized by US taxpayers through corporate expense deductions for tax purposes. Consequently, the US Congress amended the Internal Revenue Code to limit the deductible executive compensation to $1 million, unless it was performance based, in which case there was no limit. The change in the tax code effectively endorsed option-based compensation, leading companies to increase their use of options to compensate executives. Third, accounting rules in place until 2006 allowed companies to expense options based on the "intrinsic value method" for financial reporting purposes, where the intrinsic value equals the stock price less the exercise price. The implication is that options that are granted "at the money," meaning that their exercise price is set to equal the stock price on the grant date, have zero intrinsic value! However, their true economic value is always positive and can be substantial even for at-the-money options, because most likely the stock price will increase over time. In short, the accounting regulations allowed companies to grant options with massive values while reporting no expense.

As a result of options' suitability as an incentive mechanism combined with their tax and accounting benefits, the use of options increased steadily in the 1990s. By 2000, about three-quarters of large US firms used options as part of their executive compensation, and, perhaps more telling, option grants represented as much as 70 percent of total executive compensation.

The Option Granting Process

Before discussing how option grants can be manipulated, we need to cover some basics about the grant process. A firm's stock option plan, which is updated every few years and approved by the firm's shareholders, provides general guidelines. Formally, the compensation committee of the corporate board oversees the implementation, but the committee often accepts input and advice from both executives and outside compensation consultants. Options are typically granted once a year, though there might be more than one grant in a year or no grants in a year. The grants might occur on the same (or almost the same) date every year or in the same month in each year, or they might vary widely from year to year. The most common maturity, meaning the time until the options can no longer be exercised, is ten years, followed by five and seven years. Furthermore, the options typically cannot be exercised for at least a year, and sometimes up to five years.

The options are generally granted at the money, according to the option plan guidelines. This is very important for the manipulation we'll get to, although the reasons for selecting the current stock price as the exercise price are less important in our context. Anyway, there must be an exercise price, and what's more natural to select than the current stock price? This ensures that executives profit from the stock options only if the stock price increases. Furthermore, to qualify as performance-based compensation under the tax code and receive favorable tax treatment, the options cannot be granted "in the money" (meaning that they can't have an exercise price that is lower than the current stock price). Lastly, at-the-money options have no intrinsic value, allowing the companies to record no compensation expense under the accounting rules prior to 2006. This is particularly appealing to startups with weak earnings.

A final important aspect relates to the reporting of the option grants to outsiders. Firms must report option grants in the proxy statements they send to shareholders before their annual meetings. But the proxy statements are released months after the end of the fiscal year, meaning that the grant information in the proxy statements is between a few months and more than a year old. Executives are also personally responsible for reporting insider transactions, including options they have been granted. Before August 2002, executives would generally file their grants with a delay of at least one month, if they bothered to file at all, as there was seemingly no adverse consequence from the failure to do so. Starting in August 2002, the SEC required that executives file within two days.[2] Most executives complied in the subsequent years, but there were also many late filings, sloppy filings (filings with errors), and failures to file altogether, again with little consequence. This filing delay seems like a mundane detail, but it's important for the ability to manipulate option grants and for proving manipulation later.

Manipulation of Option Grants

Now we have the necessary backdrop for thinking about how option grants can be manipulated, so let's brainstorm as if we were villains. Suppose that the number of options to be granted in a year is predetermined and that the exercise price will equal the stock price on the grant day. How can we inflate the value of the grant? One strategy resembles insider trading in that we would use insider information to predict stock price movements. If we know that the company will soon release some good news, we should expedite the grant to occur before the news release to lock in a relatively low exercise price, a practice sometimes referred to as "spring-loading." Conversely, if we know that the company will soon release some bad news, we should delay the grant to occur after the news release, a practice sometimes referred to as "bullet-dodging."

A second strategy is to manipulate the information flow to the marketplace. This might be useful if the grant is scheduled ahead of time to occur on a certain date and executives have discretion in the timing of news releases. For example, if we can choose when to release bad news, it would be more opportune to do so before a scheduled grant than after.

A third strategy is to choose a grant date from the recent past, the "lookback period," when the price was particularly low, a strategy referred to as "backdating." Naturally, the longer the lookback period, the lower prices we're likely to find. But the lookback period will always be constrained. For example, we typically can't pretend to have granted the options in the prior fiscal year, because the financial statements from that year should have already reflected that grant.[3] We observed something similar to backdating in Chapter 3, where some investors were allowed to trade on stale prices, and in Chapter 4, where Madoff fabricated transactions based on past prices.

To use an analogy, if the first two manipulation strategies are akin to having an information edge when betting on future sports games, the backdating strategy is like betting on sports games that took place *in the past*. Clearly, the latter is easier because it relies on perfect hindsight instead of imperfect predictions. However, backdating option grants is possible only when the grants don't have to be filed with the SEC in a timely manner. Further, it might require some document forging and deceptive behavior to convince others that the grant decisions were made in the past. I imagine the conversation between an executive and a board member leading up to the backdating as follows:

Board member: The board has decided to give you some stock options so that you can buy stock anytime you want within the next ten years.

Executive: Yippee! But at what price?

Board member: Well, today's price is $12, so let's make it that.

Executive: You mean that even if the price increases to $100, I can still buy at $12?

Board member: Yep.

Executive: Great! But given that the price was $9 last Wednesday, could we pretend that I got the options then so that I can buy at $9 instead?

Board member: I guess. Why not? We'll find a way to provide the necessary documentation.

To be fair, board members might not be fully complicit. In many cases, the members of the compensation committee might simply sign off on paperwork related to option grants without realizing that the underlying options are backdated. In other cases, they might receive options with the same grant dates and prices as those of the executives, perhaps as an incentive for them not to interfere.

The Legality of Grant Date Manipulation

Owning a Ferrari is perfectly legal. But these high-performance machines are engineered for speed, and their owners frequently test those capabilities. So, I bet that a Ferrari is far more likely to exceed speed limits than a random Honda Civic. After all, what's the point of having such a powerful car if you don't unleash its potential?

In principle, backdating is also legal as long as several conditions hold: (i) no documents are forged as part of the process, (ii) it is clearly communicated to shareholders, (iii) it complies with shareholder-approved option plans, including restrictions against in-the-money grants, (iv) it is properly reflected in earnings, and (v) it is properly reflected in taxes, meaning that it isn't used to disguise in-the-money grants as at-the-money grants to qualify as performance-based compensation with tax benefits. Phew. That is like a user agreement for software that no one bothers to read. And come to think of it, if firms must adhere to these conditions, there's not much use in backdating anymore.

So, to me, catching someone having backdated is like catching someone at night with a lockpick and a crowbar—not illegal in itself, but it certainly raises suspicions.

What we've observed in practice is that firms that backdate rarely meet the conditions for legal use. Consequently, backdating exposes firms and their executives or board members to criminal lawsuits and civil lawsuits from the SEC and shareholders. The firms also have to restate earnings and pay additional taxes, fines, and legal expenses.

The Early Evidence of Grant Date Manipulation

In the mid-1990s, David Yermack of New York University was the first researcher to document some peculiar stock price patterns around option grants. He concentrated on what we call *abnormal* stock return, which is the difference between the total stock return and the return on the whole stock market, where the stock market serves as the benchmark. This benchmarking method, which you've encountered in previous chapters, isolates price movements unique to individual companies. If corporate insiders have inside information about future stock returns, it should pertain to the abnormal portion. Yermack found an average abnormal stock return of 2 to 3 percent during the couple of months after 620 grants from the early 1990s. He attributed most of this abnormal return to spring-loading, where option grants are strategically timed before anticipated price increases, although he did not use this specific term.

I picked up the threads in early 2003. Based on a sample of thousands of grants from 1992 to 2002, I found that the stock prices tended to decline prior to the grants. Furthermore, I noticed that the post-grant abnormal stock return that Yermack documented had intensified over time. By the end of the 1990s, the aggregate abnormal return pattern had become so pronounced that I was astounded. It looked like the letter *V* or a seagull in flight seen from the front. I grew confident that there was more to the story than just grants being timed before corporate insiders predicted stock prices would increase.

To get further clues, I divided the sample into two categories: grants that occur on roughly the same date every year, which I labeled *scheduled grants*, versus grants that occur on different dates from year to year, which I labeled *unscheduled grants*. Most of the grant timing should have been concentrated in the sample of unscheduled grants, so focusing on those grants would help me figure out what was happening.

What I found was that the pattern for the unscheduled grants was even stronger. You can see the abnormal returns during the weeks before and after the grants for yourself in Figure 8-2. The stock price declines almost 4 percent on average during the thirty trading days before the unscheduled grants, and it bounces back entirely during the subsequent thirty trading days. The sharp trough on exactly the grant day is remarkable. Could it really be that corporate insiders are that good at predicting prices? That is, could they possibly predict with such accuracy when prices will decline and bounce back again? Or did corporate insiders simply backdate the grants?

I tried one more thing. Recall that the abnormal return is the difference between the actual return and the market return, and so far, the focus had been on the abnormal return. Well, I also decided to examine the patterns in the market returns around the grants. I found that the market returns exhibited a similar pattern around grant dates as the abnormal returns: the market returns were unusually poor leading up to

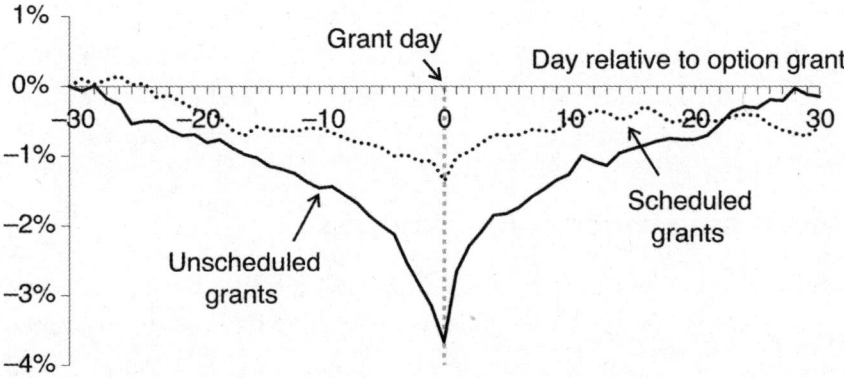

Figure 8-2. Abnormal stock returns before and after option grants.

the grants and unusually good after. I concluded that this must mean one of two things:

- corporate insiders are capable of predicting future market returns and use this ability to set grant dates to coincide with predicted troughs in the overall stock market, or

- corporate insiders backdate the grants to occur at troughs in the stock prices of the firms, irrespective of whether those troughs are due to overall market factors or firm-specific factors.

I don't believe that corporate insiders are good at predicting overall market movements—if they had that skill, they would manage hedge funds and make far more money. In fact, I don't think corporate insiders can even predict abnormal stock returns for their own firms with great accuracy. Thus, I was strongly leaning toward the second explanation that firms were backdating grants. And for the return patterns to be as strong as we saw, the practice must have been widespread.

As I was finishing this study in early 2004, I read in the *Wall Street Journal* that the SEC was investigating the possibility that some option grants were spring-loaded. I subsequently contacted the SEC, informed them about my findings, and suggested that they investigate the possibility of widespread backdating instead. Per the SEC's request, I also sent them a copy of my unpublished study and some underlying data. Then the SEC pursued its own investigation into the matter.

My paper was accepted for publication in the summer of 2004, and it was published the following year. But I don't think that anybody outside of academia paid attention to it—or was even aware of it—just yet.

More Evidence on Backdating

While the SEC was busy on their end, I still felt that there were some loose ends to tie up. I had already noted in a footnote to my initial study that the SEC introduced new filing requirements in August 2002 that should constrain the ability of firms to backdate. Consequently, I wanted to test whether the stock return patterns around option grants changed after August 2002. If backdating explained the return patterns, I expected that the pattern would diminish as executives filed their grants within two days. But if bullet-dodging, spring-loading, or manipulation of the information flow explained the return patterns, there would be no reason for the filing lag to affect the return pattern, and the return pattern should persist after August 2002. So, this might be the chance to settle the explanation once and for all.

At the end of 2004, I reached out to my good friend and long-time research collaborator, Randy Heron at Indiana University, to see if he would be willing to pursue this with me. Randy and I first got to know each other well when we shared an office in the PhD program at Purdue. He immediately bought my story and was eager to proceed.

In the initial stage of our investigation, we hand-collected executives' securities filings, available on the SEC website, and compared the grant information in individual filings to what the companies published in their proxy statements. We quickly learned that there were many missing individual filings and many inconsistencies due to executives' sloppiness when making the filings. It also became apparent that no one verified that executives made timely and accurate filings. Then we scaled up the effort by purchasing an electronic database with the individual filings. Before analyzing the data, we cleaned it up and fixed inconsistencies.

We started our analysis of the data by showing that the new filing requirements significantly affected the filing lags. For example, the fraction of filings that occurred within two days of the grants increased from a trivial portion before August 2002 to about 80 percent afterward. Then we showed that the new filing requirements had a dramatic effect on the stock return patterns. As expected, the pattern was much weaker after the filing requirement took place. Furthermore, for those that complied with the two-day filing requirement, the pattern was essentially gone, just barely visible within the couple of days of the grant when backdating might still work. We viewed this as strong evidence that backdating explains most, if not all, of the return patterns around option grants.

Now we had completely convinced ourselves that backdating of option grants had occurred on a massive scale. But we still had not convinced others.

Publishing the Coauthored Paper

Randy and I believed we had a provocative story backed up by compelling evidence. In July 2005, we submitted our manuscript to the *Journal of Finance*, and we received a report back in the beginning of September. Unfortunately, the anonymous referee butchered our paper:

> *This paper is purely descriptive and I found the research question to be poorly motivated. Moreover, interpretation of results is overreaching and makes little economic sense. Specifically, the authors conclude that the disappearance of the pattern in 2003 and 2004 is because boards stopped violating the law by granting option ex-post. I believe that a more plausible economic explanation for the authors' results is that the failure of major corporations during that period (Enron, WorldCom, etc.) and the burst of the internet bubble drew immense regulatory and investor scrutiny to executives' actions. Clearly, executives would be reluctant to go to jail for timing their options grants, an exercise that might increase their compensation by $10,000 to $50,000. Moreover, the authors take as a given that the only reason for the pattern is the backdating of options. I find this argument very shaky. The idea that most directors in the United States deliberately violate their firms charter and possibly face both class action suits and SEC criminal investigations in order to backdate options makes little economic sense.*

Having developed thick skin from many years in academia, we were outraged but only mildly discouraged.[4] We strongly disagreed with the assessment and submitted the manuscript to the *Journal of Financial Economics* instead. Fortunately, the report that we received at the end of September 2005 was more promising. But we still had a hurdle in that the referee requested more anecdotal evidence. Specifically, the referee's most critical comment was the following:

> *Though the paper presents an interesting case for backdating, it relies entirely on circumstantial evidence. The paper would improve considerably if the authors had direct, real-world evidence of the practice—this might include news stories, SEC enforcement complaints, tax court cases, private securities fraud lawsuits, and so forth. Most types of compensation shenanigans are reported from time to time in* the Wall Street Journal *and are complained about loudly by institutional investors. To my knowledge (and I follow this issue very closely), there's no public record at all related to backdating of option awards. Can the authors come up with anything?*

We were able to identify several allegations of backdating. For example, the SEC filed a complaint in 2003 against Peregrine Systems Inc., alleging that the option plan administrator at Peregrine used a lookback process between quarterly board meetings to select the day with the lowest stock price as the grant date, and that, consequently, Peregrine had understated compensation expenses by $90 million. Moreover, we got lucky in that the widespread investigation into backdating that the SEC started in 2004 began to surface. In particular, the *Wall Street Journal* (WSJ) reported on November 3, 2005, that the SEC had identified forty-nine instances at Mercury Interactive Corp. in which option grant dates were determined on a backdated basis and that Mercury Interactive's new executive believed that the SEC had inquired into the option-accounting practice of thirty to forty other Silicon Valley firms.[5] With these anecdotes, the manuscript was accepted for publication.

The *Wall Street Journal* Takes Over

On the same day that the WSJ published the article about Mercury Interactive, Randy sent an email on our behalf to the three journalists who wrote the article. The email outlined our evidence of widespread backdating and offered our assistance in understanding the issue. One of the journalists, Mark Maremont, showed great interest and published an article in the WSJ the following week that described the practice of backdating option grants and the relevant academic research.

However, as an experienced journalist with an eye for scandals, Mark wanted to pursue this further. Despite our reluctance to name and shame, I supplied him with some data that helped identify which companies were most likely to have backdated option grants. Over the next several months, the WSJ dedicated substantial resources to investigating backdating of option grants among US corporations. Led by Charles Forelle, a team of journalists gathered more grant data and talked to people in academia and business. This led to the publication of the article titled "The Perfect Payday" on March 18, 2006, surely one of the WSJ's most important and influential articles ever. The article identified six companies that were highly likely to have backdated option grants, which, in turn, triggered several events among the identified companies, including ousters of top executives, restatements of earnings, class action lawsuits, and criminal investigations.

Over the next year, the WSJ identified more companies that had likely backdated options and gave regular updates on the scandal as it spread across corporate America. In the end, hundreds of companies were entangled in the scandal, though a lot of the entanglement, including some lawsuits, were kept out of the public eye.

In 2007, the WSJ was awarded the Pulitzer Prize for Public Service "for its creative and comprehensive probe into backdated stock options for business executives that triggered investigations, the ouster of top officials and widespread change in corporate America." The Pulitzer Prize for Public Service is the only Pulitzer Prize that comes with a gold medal and is the most coveted among newspapers. It was the first time, and still the only time, that the WSJ has won this prestigious award.

The Regulators and Legislators Respond

In July 2006, the SEC altered the reporting rules on executive compensation by, for example, requiring disclosure of (i) the closing market price on the grant date if it exceeds the exercise price, (ii) the date the compensation committee or full board of directors made the grant if that date differs from the grant date, and (iii) the methodology for determining the exercise price if the exercise price differs from the grant date closing market price.

Two congressional hearings followed in September 2006, giving politicians on Capitol Hill a welcome chance to castigate greed in the executive rank. In the Senate Banking Committee, I testified along with Chris Cox, chairman of the SEC, and Mark Olson, chairman of PCAOB. In the Senate Finance Committee, Mark Everson, commissioner of the IRS, witnessed.

Case Studies

The academic research was designed to uncover broad trends rather than identify specific companies. In fact, none of the academic studies identified specific companies based on the data. Nevertheless, when companies repeatedly and egregiously backdated option grants, it is possible to single them out as likely offenders.

Conversely, if the companies were more cautious in their behavior, perhaps by only backdating some of their grants or by not picking the date with the very lowest price as the grant date, it is difficult, if not impossible, to prove backdating based on stock prices and grant data alone. There are many anecdotes of such caution. For example, Brocade Communications Systems adopted a practice of avoiding the date with the lowest price from the lookback period as the grant date, instead picking a date when the price was relatively low. And even a child understands not to take all the remaining cookies from the jar to avoid getting caught.

The six companies that the WSJ identified in its Perfect Payday article were all outliers, exhibiting repetitive and egregious backdating. Figures 8-3 and 8-4 show the stock prices of two of these companies, Comverse Technology and UnitedHealth Group, along with their option grant dates. Even to the naked eye, it is evident that the grants repeatedly coincide with troughs in stock prices. But is it possible that the executives just got very lucky?

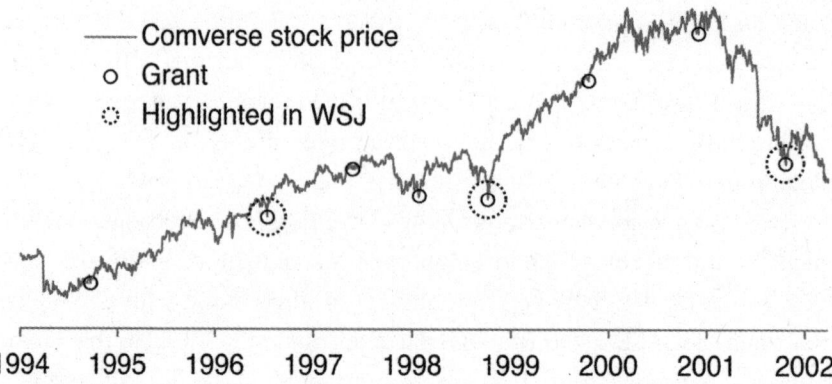

Figure 8-3. The stock prices and option grants of Comverse Technology.

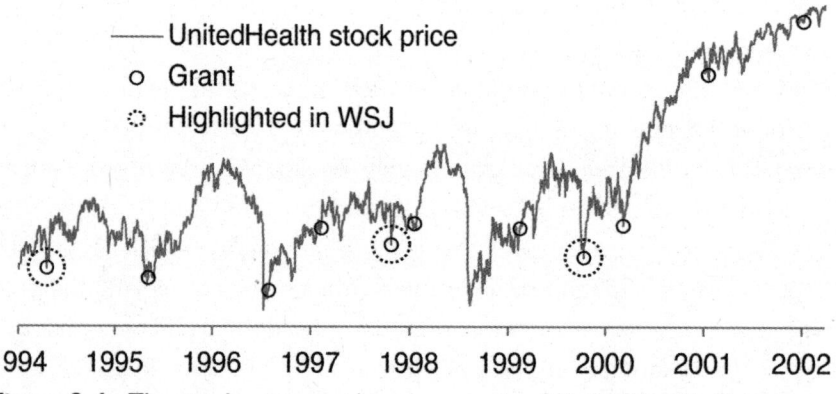

Figure 8-4. The stock prices and option grants of UnitedHealth Group.

We can use various methods to estimate the probability that the grant dates coincide with dates with such low prices purely by chance. Common to all methods is that they require a reasonable assumption about what the possible lookback period was, such as the month or fiscal quarter of the grant. We can then use the binomial distribution to estimate the probability that a certain number of grants occurred at the lowest price (or one of the lowest prices) during the lookback period.[6] Personally, though, I like to run simulations to estimate this probability. For example, I might simulate one million hypothetical grants and examine how often the simulated grants are as "lucky" as the actual grants. This is a little trickier to implement, but very powerful and more flexible in dealing with some of the firms' defenses (which I'll outline in a moment).

With the help of a statistician, the WSJ relied on the binomial distribution to estimate that the probabilities that the sets of grant dates for Comverse Technology and UnitedHealth Group coincided with such low stock prices were both less than one in a hundred million. In other words, luck alone could not possibly explain the patterns in the graphs for these two companies.

Firms that showed a suspicious pattern for the timing of their grant dates had several common defenses. The most common defense was that option recipients were simply very lucky. While this explanation might be reasonable in many cases, it doesn't hold up in extreme cases like the ones described earlier. Another related defense was that, among thousands of firms, some are bound to be very lucky. Therefore, if an investigator searches through all firms for potential culprits, they will inevitably find some that appear suspicious, even if no backdating occurred. To counter this, we need to focus on firms with odds more extreme than one in thousands, unless there is another reason to suspect a particular firm, such as shared board members or geographic proximity to another firm known to be guilty of backdating. Yet another defense was that the firm had a practice of granting options after stock prices had fallen, which would explain why the grant dates tended to coincide with low prices. The academic research certainly did not support this explanation in the aggregate. But to guard against this possibility for individual firms, we must conduct an analysis that focuses solely on the positive returns after the grants and disregards the negative returns before the grants.

To get a better sense of the backdating process and gain, let's zoom in on Comverse Technology's option grant to CEO Kobi Alexander in October 1998, one of three grants highlighted in the WSJ. The number of shares subject to option was 250,000 and the exercise price was $30, which was the lowest price for fiscal year 1998. Given a fiscal year-end price of $84, the intrinsic value of the options at the end of the year was ($84 – $30) × 250,000 = $13,500,000. In comparison, had the options been granted at the year-end price when the decision to grant the options might have been made, the year-end intrinsic value would have been zero. So, Alexander was better off by millions of dollars as a result of the fortuitous timing.

Let's also zoom in on UnitedHealth's option grant to CEO Bill McGuire in October 1999, which is another grant that the WSJ highlighted. The number of shares subject to option was 1,825,000 and the exercise price was $40.125, which was the lowest price for fiscal year 1999. Given a year-end price of $53.125, the intrinsic value of the options at the end of the year was ($53.125 – $40.125) × 1,825,000 = $23,725,000. No wonder the WSJ called it a perfect payday!

The WSJ disclosures triggered a series of events, both in the companies that the WSJ outed and in other companies, and it would take a separate book to describe all of them. I will merely summarize what happened to the CEOs at Comverse and UnitedHealth.

The rise and fall of Kobi Alexander, the founder and CEO of Comverse, is worthy of a feature-length film. Alexander, an Israeli citizen, founded Comverse in the early 1980s and turned it into a leading maker of telecommunications software with the help of Israeli government subsidies and tax credits. But he was also allegedly the mastermind of a backdating scheme, personally realizing more than $100 million from backdated options.

After the WSJ contacted Comverse on March 3, 2006, Alexander and other executives tried to hide the backdating scheme by lying to a company lawyer, misleading auditors, and altering computer records. Alexander also attempted to bribe another person $5 million to take the fall and wired $57 million to Israel before the US authorities froze $48 million of his assets. Then Alexander and his family traveled to Namibia via Israel.

In Namibia, Alexander and his family established a new life safe from US prosecutors, as Namibia has no formal extradition treaty with the US. He transferred millions of dollars from Israel to Namibia, bought a half-million-dollar house facing a golf course in the capital, and hired a security guard to stand outside the house. To cultivate local goodwill, he invested in local businesses and donated generously to, for example, a local synagogue, a low-income housing project, and a soup kitchen.

In 2010, a class action lawsuit against Comverse, Alexander, and other former officers and directors was settled for $225 million. The settlement called for a $60 million recovery from Alexander.

In 2016, Alexander returned to the US after having negotiated a plea agreement that protected his assets and required him to plead to only one criminal count, down from more than thirty counts in the original indictment. He was sentenced to thirty months in prison.

And then we have Bill McGuire, the highly regarded CEO of the giant health insurer UnitedHealth. Under his tenure, UnitedHealth grew its annual revenues from less than $0.5 billion to more than $70 billion, for which he was compensated close to $2 billion. His philanthropy and generosity produced tremendous goodwill both in the community, with gifts of $10 million each to Walker Art Center and Guthrie Theatre in Minneapolis, and in the board of directors, with donations to charities in which the directors were involved.

The board gave McGuire broad latitude to grant options to subordinates and to choose the timing of option grants to himself. Formally, the compensation committee also had to approve the grant dates, but there were no records to show that the options were approved on recorded grant dates, and minutes of compensation committee meetings were mysteriously missing. By the end of 2005, McGuire had accumulated unexercised options worth $1.8 billion, far more than the value of unexercised options held by any other CEO in the country.

McGuire agreed to resign as CEO and surrender more than $600 million(!) in stock option gains and retirement pay to settle civil and federal claims related to backdating. Furthermore, UnitedHealth settled for more than $900 million to resolve shareholder lawsuits.

In an interesting twist, investors also found a way to use the ordinarily dull bond market to make money on the backdating debacle. Corporate bond contracts generally obligate the issuer to file quarterly reports in a timely manner with the SEC to avoid technical default. When a group of opportunistic investors recognized that (i) UnitedHealth's backdating problems would delay its SEC filings and (ii) UnitedHealth's bonds were trading at a discount relative to their face value, the investors bought a bunch of its $800 million bonds due in 2036. When UnitedHealth indeed failed to file its second quarterly report for 2006, the investors promptly wrote a letter on August 25, 2006, in which they demanded immediate payment unless the filing was made within sixty days. Pretty clever, right?

A Widespread Practice

The previous graphs show negative returns before option grants followed by positive returns afterward. Most prominently, before 2002, the average abnormal return in the weeks before unscheduled grants is –4 percent, and afterward it is +4 percent. This couldn't possibly be explained by just a few isolated incidents of backdating. Rather, it suggests backdating on a massive scale. For example, if only 1 percent of the grants were backdated, they would have to be associated with an average pre-grant return of –400 percent and a post-grant return of 400 percent, both of which are impossibly large.[7] And if 10 percent of the grants were backdated, they would have to be associated with an average pre-grant return of –40 percent and a post-grant return of 40 percent, which also seem highly unlikely. So, more than 10 percent of the grants must have been backdated.

Randy and I took a different approach by comparing the stock returns during the twenty trading days before and after the grants. In the absence of manipulation, the returns should be similar in both periods, meaning the probability of returns being higher after the grants should be around 50 percent. But what happens if backdating is involved?

Suppose that 20 percent of the grants are backdated, resulting in higher returns after the grants compared to before. In addition, half of the 80 percent non-backdated grants also have greater returns afterward. Therefore, 20 percent + 40 percent = 60 percent exhibit higher returns after the grants. By reverse engineering this logic, we can deduce that if 60 percent of the grants show higher returns afterward, about 20 percent of them must have been backdated.

Based on this reasoning, we estimated that nearly 30 percent of firms that granted options to top executives between 1996 and 2005 manipulated one or more of these grants. This equates to over two thousand publicly traded US firms! How could we have been unaware of this for so long?

Extensions: Exercises and Gifts

The basic methodology presented here can be applied to other transactions by corporate executives as well, and several subsequent academic studies have examined manipulation of other transaction dates. I'll give two examples in which US taxpayers ended up with the bill.

David Cicero examined exercises of options among US executives, noting that many executives retain the shares they acquire upon exercising these options. Why would the stock price of the shares on the exercise date matter then? The short answer is to reduce their taxes. Executives must pay ordinary income taxes on the difference between the stock price and the exercise price, while they pay capital gains taxes on any subsequent price appreciation when they eventually sell the shares. Because the latter tax is generally smaller and paid later than the former, executives would prefer for the stock price to be low on the exercise date. Consistent with the idea that executives manipulate the exercise date to minimize their tax burden, the prices on the exercise dates for these transactions tend to be abnormally low, just like they are for option grant dates.

David Yermack studied a sample of 150 stock gifts of at least $1 million by CEOs and board chairmen to their own family foundations. He hypothesized that the gift dates were manipulated to coincide with dates on which the stock prices were particularly high to inflate the value of the tax deduction. Indeed, the gifts tended to occur at peaks in the stock prices, especially when the filing lag was long. Yermack concluded that executives backdated gifts to minimize their tax burden. And, yes,

Yermack pointed out the irony that executives both gave to charities and cheated the government in the same transaction, titling his paper "Deductio' ad absurdum."

History Repeats Itself: Kodak during the Pandemic

Since the advent of digital cameras, sales of film for photography and movies have plummeted to almost nothing. Eastman Kodak Co., once the industry leader, struggled to adapt and ultimately filed for bankruptcy in 2012. The following year, Kodak reorganized and emerged from bankruptcy as a smaller company, shifting its focus to commercial customers.

When the coronavirus created havoc in the United States during the second quarter of 2020, Kodak recognized an opportunity for its little-known pharmaceutical unit. It boosted its lobbying efforts and reached out to the Trump administration and the US International Development Finance Corporation (DFC). Typically, the DFC makes loans in developing countries, but during the pandemic, it was charged with making business loans under the Defense Production Act. Kodak's efforts appeared to pay off; it came close to finalizing a $765 million loan from the DFC to set up operations that would help manufacture pharmaceuticals to fight the coronavirus. On July 28, President Trump announced the deal with Kodak as if it were finalized. The stock price of Kodak skyrocketed from less than $3 to an intraday peak of $60 on July 29, as Figure 8-5 indicates. However, when investors discovered in the subsequent days that the deal might not go through, Kodak's price fell precipitously.

Kodak took investors for a wild roller-coaster ride around the deal announcement, including new day traders using the Robinhood app, some of whom vowed never to invest in Kodak again afterward. Meanwhile, insiders at Kodak exploited the massive volatility.

On July 27, before the spectacular price increase, CEO Jim Continenza received an option grant for 1.75 million shares. The grant was supposedly based on an "understanding" with the board of directors and

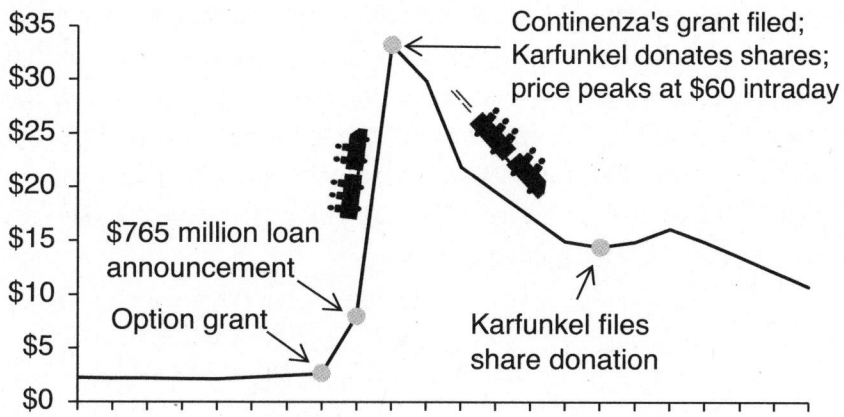

Figure 8-5. The roller-coaster ride of Kodak's stock price.

was never formalized or made public in advance. Furthermore, the grant was not filed until July 29, when the stock price hit its intraday peak of $60. This has all the markings of backdating; it was filed with a lag after a dramatic increase in the stock price and it was hidden from the public until the filing. If it were indeed backdated, Continenza received a windfall of roughly $50 million, far exceeding his base salary of $1 million.

Board member George Karfunkel appears to have engaged in some different improprieties. On July 25, he owned 6.3 million Kodak shares, which, given a price of $2.62, were worth $16.5 million. On July 27, Karfunkel donated three million of his Kodak shares to a Jewish synagogue in New York where he served as the congregation's president. Using the IRS valuation method, which averages the low ($17.50) and high ($60) prices of the day to get $38.75, the donation was worth $116.3 million, making it the largest gift on record to a religious organization. This donation could be claimed as a tax deduction, likely worth tens of millions.

While this initially appears to be a generous act rewarded with a significant tax break, there is reason to be suspicious: the donation was not filed until August 4, four trading days after the alleged donation date, despite security rules requiring such disclosures to be made "promptly," which SEC guidance suggests is within two trading days. The delayed filing combined with the enormous price drop between the alleged transaction and filing dates also have the markings of backdating. Had the gift date instead been changed to the filing date, the value of the tax break would be more than halved. The fortuitous timing of the gift not only portrayed Karfunkel as a record-generous man but also gave him a tax break that exceeded the value of the shares before the loan announcement. Crafty, indeed.

Epilogue

Sunlight is said to be the best of disinfectants;
electric light the most efficient policeman.

—LOUIS D. BRANDEIS, Supreme Court Justice

Corporate fraud impedes economic progress, hinders equitable allocation of resources, fosters poverty, contributes to environmental pollution and global warming, and taints our culture. This book offers no prescription for eradicating fraud. But it demonstrates how data can be used to expose systematic fraud, which is the first step for addressing the underlying issues. It also underscores the societal value of accessible data combined with a free press and an active research community.

There is compelling evidence that increased scrutiny helps reduce fraud. For instance, researchers Vivian Fang, Allen Huang, and Jonathan Karpoff found that when the SEC temporarily lifted short-selling constraints for a random set of stocks, making it easier for investors to bet against companies, those firms curbed their earnings management. Those that failed to do so faced a higher likelihood of being caught. This shows that investors, driven by their financial incentives, play a crucial role in disciplining companies. We also know from other research that firms caught for financial misconduct incur huge costs from reputational damage, so executives logically fear and respond to scrutiny.

Figure 1. Illuminating fraud.

I'll conclude with a last example that shows how private citizens can help, especially when incentivized. During the pandemic in 2020, the federal government launched the $800 billion Paycheck Protection Program (PPP) to encourage small businesses to keep their workers on the payroll. To expedite the distribution of the relief funds, much of the traditional vetting was waived. In 2021, researchers John Griffin, Samuel Kruger, and Prateek Mahajan uncovered numerous indicators of fraud in the data, including nonregistered businesses, multiple loans issued to the same residential address, unusually high compensation compared to industry standards, and significant discrepancies between the jobs reported on PPP applications and those reported on other government program applications. For instance, fifteen different businesses, each with exactly ten employees and all located in the same modest suburban Chicago home, received loans. Twelve of these loans were for $53,229, while the others were for $53,125, $62,083, and $91,770. The clustering of locations, especially when combined with the clustering of the employee numbers and the loan amounts, should have raised serious flags.

Later estimates indicate that thousands of fraudulent actors seized a staggering $200 billion of the PPP funds. However, limited resources have prevented federal investigators from pursuing reimbursements. Consequently, private citizens have entered the fray. Under the False Claims Act, they can file lawsuits on behalf of the government and keep 15 to 30 percent of the recovered funds. As a result, private citizens have scoured public data sources in search of the same fraud patterns as academic researchers and supplemented with social media data to build individual cases, earning them hundreds of thousands of dollars or more.

Systematic fraud inevitably leaves behind a trail of data crumbs that attentive and skilled individuals can recognize. Having finished this book, I encourage you to bring out your own flashlight and help illuminate fraud, as in Figure 1. The pursuit is on.

Notes

Chapter 2

1   At some random times in March 2021, I looked up spreads of popular stocks among Robinhood traders. The quoted spread for Apple was consistently below 0.01 percent, and it ranged from 0.01 percent to 0.08 percent for Tesla, 0.07 percent to 0.14 percent for AMC Entertainment, and 0.07 percent to 0.8 percent for GameStop. Sundial Growers (a cannabis company) mostly had a spread of a penny, representing a hefty 0.7 percent of its low price of about $1.50. For less liquid stocks, the spreads could be much wider. But if you actually place a trade, you are likely to get a price inside the quoted spread. Thus, it is hard to ascertain exactly what cost the spread will represent in a trade.

2   In 2021, the dozen largest US brokerages, including Charles Schwab and Robinhood, earned $3.8 billion from selling their customers' orders (a practice called "payment for order flow") to trading firms. Of this, Citadel Securities paid $1.5 billion. (Citadel Securities is owned by billionaire Ken Griffin, known for his art collection, trophy homes, huge contributions to the Republican Party, and the naming gift to the renowned Department of Economics at the University of Chicago.) Citadel and other trading firms claim that they secure better prices for investors than what conventional stock exchanges offer. But others disagree, and the SEC is pushing for more competition in the trading of securities.

3   In September 2024, the SEC approved a change that would allow many stock prices to be quoted in increments of half-cents.

4 In 1997, the US Congress tried to pass the bill with the clever name Common Cents Stock Pricing Act, which would have required that US stock markets trade on dollars and cents, but the bill failed to pass.

5 Alert readers might recognize that in this analysis, Christie and Schultz employ both forensic methods introduced in the prior chapter. Their expectation was that the quotes should be evenly distributed across even and odd eighths, which does not hold for NASDAQ stocks, suggesting some type of disruption in the distribution. Furthermore, they used the quotes for NYSE/AMEX stocks as a benchmark for the quotes for NASDAQ stocks and found a significant difference. Both methods lead to the conclusion that the NASDAQ stock quotes are highly irregular.

6 Plaintiff law firms often maintain ongoing relationships with institutional investors such as pension funds. These pension funds, being long-term shareholders in many companies, are likely to have owned shares in the target company (in this case, various investment banks) during the relevant period. When the plaintiff law firms identify a potential target for a class action lawsuit, they reach out to the pension fund to be the lead plaintiff, sometimes paying illegal kickbacks or making dubious donations to politicians who have influence over the institutional investors.

Chapter 3

1 For example, an investment banker might be tempted to ask an analyst to issue a buy recommendation for a firm so that the investment banker can gain/retain that firm as a client. A "Chinese Wall" between the investment bankers who provide services to outside firms and the analysts who analyze those very same firms mitigates such corrupt behavior.

2 In contrast, trades of exchange traded funds (ETFs), a more recent development of pooling securities and a direct competitor to the more traditional mutual funds, occur instantly at prices that are determined in the marketplace and change continuously. Thus, trading in ETFs is just like trading in stocks, and ETFs are not susceptible to the trading games explained in this chapter. There are also tax advantages to choosing ETFs over mutual funds, but that's beyond the scope of this discussion.

3 There are, however, less noble reasons for mutual funds to charge redemption fees and limit trades, including steadier investment levels and the prevention of outflows.

4 In Harrington's next job as chief investment officer of the hedge fund Sterling Stamos, she assessed a possible investment in Bernie Madoff's hedge fund (more on that fund and its collapse in Chapter 4). Sterling Stamos was co-owned by Fred Wilpon and Saul Katz, who at the time also owned the New York Mets before selling to billionaire Steven Cohen, a key player in Chapter 6. After some due diligence, Harrington conveyed to Wilpon and Katz in 2003 that Madoff's hedge fund returns were too good to be true and strongly recommended against the investment. Katz, a friend of Madoff, got visibly angry, and the partners ignored Harrington's warning. In response, Harrington resigned.

5 Here are some numbers to help you digest these concepts. Suppose that a mutual fund with one million shares has a true value of $200 million ($200 per share), but its NAV is only $190 million ($190 per share) because of the stale prices used in the calculation. Now, imagine a trader is allowed to buy 100,000 shares at the stale NAV for a total purchase price of $19 million. Immediately afterward, the mutual fund has the old portfolio worth $200 million plus $19 million in cash, and the number of shares has increased to 1.1 million. The updated true value per share is then $219 million / 1.1 million shares = $199.09. In other words, the long-term investors lost $0.91 / $200 = 0.5% on this deal.

6 For that reason, mutual funds market their good past performance—they should be able to identify at least some period during which their performance was good—in their marketing material to encourage more inflow.

7 Interestingly, Andrew Cuomo replaced Spitzer as the attorney general and served in that position for one term until he became the governor in 2011. But on August 3, 2021, the attorney general of New York released a report that Cuomo had sexually harassed eleven women during his time in office. Faced with almost certain removal from office, Cuomo resigned as governor effective August 24, 2021.

8 Bruno was later indicted for political corruption for accepting payments from private companies in exchange for state business. Stone was later convicted for obstructing a congressional investigation into President

Trump's 2016 campaign and Russian ties, but Trump commuted Stone's sentence in a highly controversial 2020 decision.

9 Banks must file Suspicious Activity Reports (SARs) to the Financial Crimes Enforcement Network (FinCEN), a division of the Treasury Department, when they suspect money laundering, terrorist financing, and other financial crimes. FinCEN maintains a secure database of the SARs that is accessible to authorized federal, state, and local enforcement agencies.

Chapter 4

1 In academia, we often refer to the excess return above benchmarks as *abnormal return* instead, and I use this term instead of *alpha* when discussing academic evidence.

2 Madoff might not have initially intended for his business to be a Ponzi scheme. Then again, neither was the scheme that Charles Ponzi concocted around 1920. Ponzi realized that international reply coupons (IRCs)—essentially stamps usable in any country—were cheaper in Italy than in the United States. Thus, he planned to buy tons of IRCs in Italy and sell them in the United States at a profit. In January 1920, he founded the Securities Exchange Company (not to be confused with the Securities and Exchange Commission, the US regulatory body founded fourteen years later) to execute his plan. With the promise of a high return, Ponzi attracted investments of $1,800 in the first month, which he promptly repaid with interest the next month. With trust established, existing investors reinvested, and new investors joined. To Ponzi, it didn't matter that the business plan turned out to be logistically impossible to implement, because money was pouring in anyway. Until August 1920, that is, when the scheme unraveled.

3 In recent years, many high-speed traders have paid brokerage firms for their business, which can create conflicts of interest in that the broker gets more interested in enhancing such payments than in getting their customers the best prices. In 2020, Robinhood Markets, Inc., whose trading app gained popularity among individual investors during the pandemic, received about $700 million in payment-for-order flow and settled for $65 million with the SEC for its failure to properly disclose such arrangements.

4 It's doubtful that the investment advisory business actually placed many, if any, trades. More likely, the money was deposited into bank accounts and used to cover operating costs.

5 *Call* options allow the holder to *buy* stock at a predetermined price called the *exercise price*. Thus, the higher the stock price goes, the more valuable the call option becomes. If you buy a call option, you essentially acquire the upside potential for the stock, thus gambling on a stock price increase, whereas if you sell a call option, you give up the upside potential. Conversely, *put* options allow the holder to *sell* stock at a predetermined price. Thus, the lower the stock price goes, the more valuable the put option becomes. For that reason, put options are often acquired as an insurance against stock price drops.

6 Here's a toy example. Suppose we have a diversified portfolio resembling the S&P 500 worth $10 billion. Then we sell call options on the S&P 500 with an exercise price 10 percent higher than the current S&P 500 level, such that our combined position (ignoring the proceeds from selling the call options) is limited to $11 billion. Furthermore, we use the sales proceeds to buy put options with an exercise price 10 percent below the current S&P 500 level. Now we have a combined position with a value that is guaranteed to be between $9 and $11 billion, irrespective of what happens to the S&P 500.

7 On August 15, 2019, Markopolos released a 169-page report alleging that General Electric (GE) committed accounting fraud. Given his notoriety as a whistleblower from the Madoff scandal, his allegation caused GE's price to plunge 11 percent, representing $9 billion of GE's market capitalization! But it appears that this time Markopolos was wrong, and GE gradually recovered the lost value. What made this incident suspicious was that Markopolos had given the report to a hedge fund in advance, allowing the hedge fund to short GE's stock and profit from the stock price plunge. It seems like the good guys on Wall Street are only good for so long.

8 Arvedlund later wrote the book *Too Good to Be True: The Rise and Fall of Bernie Madoff*, published in 2009.

9 Under bankruptcy law, funds that have been paid out to investors during a certain period (six years in New York State) can be clawed back to the firm for an orderly distribution to all investors, irrespective of the motive for the withdrawals.

10 Benford's Law has also been used to detect fraud in large data sets. According to this law, the digit 1 appears as the first digit about 30 percent of the time, with the frequency decreasing steadily for higher digits, reaching around 5 percent for the digit 9. Fabricated numbers often deviate from this natural distribution, thereby providing a clue. For example, in the Fairfield Sentry returns discussed earlier, 40 percent of the first digits equal the digit 1, which is 10 percent higher than what Benford's law predicts.

Chapter 5

1 Firms listed on stock exchanges are subject to Securities and Exchange (SEC) regulations and must submit their 10-K, including balance sheet and income statement, to the SEC within sixty days of the end of the fiscal year. The firms also need to follow generally accepted accounting principles (GAAP).

2 To any finance professionals who happen to be reading this book: I know that you will criticize this simplistic view and argue that it's not all about earnings, that we must discount, and so on. Nevertheless, I think you will agree that the insight from my presentation is valid.

3 More broadly, off-balance sheet financing refers to debt obligations that companies have but that do not appear on the balance sheet. Leases are another example of off-balance sheet financing because the lease obligations generally don't show up as a liability on the balance sheet.

4 Without getting into the weeds, to short-sell a stock (or just "short" a stock) means to borrow a stock and immediately sell it, with the obligation to buy it back later and turn it over to the original owner. This strategy generates a profit if the stock falls in value and the fees for borrowing the stock are modest. You will see this term being used in other parts of the book as well.

5 Ironically, George W. Bush had close ties to Enron. Ken Lay was a longtime friend of the Bush family. Furthermore, Enron was the largest financial contributor when Bush ran for governor in Texas, and Enron gave Bush access to its jet when he ran for president.

6 In September 2020, *Financial Times* journalist Dan McCrumb penned a captivating article detailing his investigation into Wirecard and the intimidation and bullying he faced from Wirecard representatives. Under the leadership of its chief operating officer, Jan Marsalek, who

had connections to the Russian secret service, Wirecard fabricated news, including false reports of a takeover, spied on McCrumb and the *Financial Times*, and accused McCrumb of conspiring with short sellers betting on the stock price falling. In response, McCrumb had to operate in secrecy, often going off the grid and using code names to confuse any moles. This story has all the elements of an action-packed Hollywood thriller.

7   In an episode of *This American Life* from 2013 called "129 Cars," journalists spent a month at a Jeep dealership on Long Island as it tried to sell 129 cars to secure a huge bonus from the manufacturer. Toward the end of the month, the employees worked long hours, slashed prices below cost, desperately called potential customers, and even bought cars for themselves or for the maintenance department to be used as loaner cars. Their efforts paid off: the dealership sold exactly 129 cars for the month—just what was needed for the bonus.

8   My favorite example of reference points comes from the used car market. More than a decade ago, I asked an acquaintance why he regularly sells his cars when the mileage reaches the high twenty thousands. His response: the price falls dramatically as the odometer rounds thirty thousand miles. While it's common knowledge that prices decrease with higher mileage, I thought it was nonsense that there is a precipitous drop right around thirty thousand miles. However, in 2012, I read an article in the *American Economic Review* titled "Heuristic Thinking and Limited Attention in the Car Market" that proved me wrong. Based on car auction data, the authors found discontinuous drops in sale prices at each ten-thousand-mile odometer threshold. They argued that this occurs because car buyers focus too much on the first digit of the odometer reading.

9   If you're interested, look up the infamous footnote 16 from Enron's 2000 annual report.

Chapter 6

1   The information does not need to be perfect. In the long run, any information that allows traders to be correct more than half the time is helpful. Roger Federer only won 54 percent of his points in his professional tennis career, yet he won twenty Grand Slam titles and is considered by many to be the greatest player of all time.

2 GLG recruited me as an expert back in 2005, and when the backdating scandal was at its peak, I received so many invitations to consult that I joined the GLG Leaders Program, which was available to the top 5 percent of members. In recent years, however, I have only received invitations to consult on matters that would require preparation time on my side, so I have rejected them. Also, I do not possess valuable insider information, so investors are less keen to speak to me.

3 Patrick Radden Keefe's 2014 *New Yorker* story titled "The Empire of Edge" about this case is by far the best insider-trading article I have read. The author went on to write *Say Nothing: A True Story of Murder and Memory in Northern Ireland*, which *Time* magazine named the best nonfiction book of 2019 and was turned into a Hulu TV series in 2024, and *Empire of Pain*, which the readers at GoodReads.com voted to be the best history/biography book of 2021.

4 Martoma claimed that he had submitted the forged transcripts in his applications for clerkships by mistake, and that he had withdrawn his applications before the forgery was discovered. He went to exceptional lengths to try to prove his version of the timeline, even setting up his own computer forensic company to conduct an analysis that his withdrawal emails had been sent several days before the timestamps on the emails.

5 The bestselling book *Black Edge: Inside Information, Dirty Money, and the Quest to Bring Down the Most Wanted Man on Wall Street* by Sheelah Kolhatkar (published in 2017) describes in detail the unsuccessful efforts to put Cohen away for insider trading. Also, the first season of the Showtime TV series *Billions* is loosely based on the pursuit of Cohen.

6 Anita Raghavan followed the Rajaratnam case as a journalist and later wrote an outstanding book called *The Billionaire's Apprentice* (published in 2011) about the case in the context of the rise of the Indian elite in the United States.

7 Almost a decade later, in 2007, the SEC found a reckless instant message from Khan to Raj revealing her access to inside information, and this helped the SEC recruit Khan as an informant against Raj. Khan was a very effective informant, but she also hid information and lied to protect certain individuals. Thus, she was sentenced to one year in prison for insider trading and obstruction of justice. She explained all of this in a *60 Minutes*

segment on CBS from 2016 called "A Rare Look at How Insider Trading Works."

8 Starting in 2003, Rajaratnam paid Kumar as an informant without inform-ing McKinsey, and Rajaratnam regularly wired money totaling several million dollars to a Swiss bank account in Kumar's housekeeper's name. Kumar provided especially valuable and confidential information to Raja-ratnam on Advanced Micro Devices, for which Kumar worked as a highly trusted consultant.

9 Milken was permanently banned from the securities industry and was sen-tenced to ten years in prison but served only twenty-two months. After his release, he became heavily involved in philanthropic activities, particularly in cancer research and education, and in 2020, he received a controversial pardon from President Trump.

10 Bachus bought ProShares UltraShort QQQ, which is designed to increase in value by twice as much as the NASDAQ 100 index decreases in value, and vice versa. For example, if the NASDAQ 100 goes down 1 percent, Pro-Shares UltraShort QQQ goes up roughly 2 percent.

11 The additional requirement that records be posted online spurred privacy and safety concerns, especially among the thousands of staffers. Thus, in 2013, the STOCK Act was quietly amended so that these staffers no longer had to file online, which made it much harder for the public to access these records.

12 The researchers also examined trades for bank insiders with no political connections, but they found no similar trend.

Chapter 7

1 This example is taken from the *Wall Street Journal* article dated April 16, 2008, titled "Libor Fog: Bankers Cast Doubt on Key Rate Amid Crisis."

2 In the graph, the peak is 3.3 percent on October 1, 2008, but daily data shows that the peak was about 4.5 percent on October 10, 2008.

3 After the pervasive LIBOR manipulation was exposed in the media, jour-nalist Matt Taibbi at *Rolling Stone* wrote that it "makes Enron look like a parking violation. . . . There is nobody anywhere growing weed strong enough to help the human mind grasp the enormity of this crime."

4 In Mollenkamp's follow-up article, he reported that "over the next two days [after the publication of the original article], banks raised their reported rates, causing dollar-denominated Libor to log its biggest jump since August." While this was true, the increase in LIBOR was likely due to an increase in Treasury yield at the same time, not to bankers being less aggressive in pushing down their submissions.

5 If CDSs are truly insurance contracts and not swaps, why not call them that? One possibility is that labeling CDSs as insurance would have subjected them to regulatory oversight. For instance, issuers might have been required to maintain capital reserves to cover large insurance payouts, which would be costly. On the flip side, this regulation might have spared us much of the devastation during the financial crisis, including the collapses of Lehman Brothers and AIG, which issued massive quantities of CDSs without sufficient financial backing.

6 Mollenkamp and Whitehouse also provided anecdotal evidence. For example, they wrote that in mid-April of 2008, UBS had offered to pay 2.85 percent for a loan yet submitted a LIBOR rate of only 2.73 percent, in line with the other panel banks.

Chapter 8

1 Conversely, *put* options allow the holder to *sell* the stock at a fixed price, but these are never used as part of executive compensation, because they would give executives the perverse incentive to drive the company into the ground.

2 The tighter filing requirement was part of the Sarbanes-Oxley Act, which was enacted in response to several major accounting scandals, including those at Enron and WorldCom (see Chapter 5). The regulators believed that tighter filing requirements were needed after, for example, Enron CEO Ken Lay sold shares for more than $100 million before Enron's stock tanked without informing market participants in a timely manner.

3 Microsoft Corp. admitted to using a lookback period of one month: it granted options at monthly lows each July from 1992 to 1999, and it also granted options to new employees at the lowest price during the thirty days after they joined.

4 I will refrain from writing what we said amongst ourselves about the referee and the report, except to say that there was some graphic language. Moreover, we have no idea where the referee got the range of "$10,000 to $50,000" from, a range that seemed far too low to us. Later, it would prove to be ridiculously low.

5 There is also some relatively early anecdotal evidence of backdating. A particularly interesting example is that of Micrel Inc. For several years, Micrel allowed its employees to choose the lowest price for the stock within thirty days of receiving the options. After these stock option terms came to the attention of the IRS in 2002, it worked out a secret deal with Micrel that would allow Micrel to escape $51 million in taxes and required the IRS to keep quiet about the option terms. Remy Welling, a senior auditor at the IRS, was asked to sign the deal in late 2002. Instead, she risked criminal prosecution by blowing the whistle. However, fearing public embarrassment, the government did not pursue legal action against Welling.

6 This is quite simple. Suppose that three of five grants occur at monthly lows. Given that there are about twenty trading days in a month, the chance of hitting the monthly low is 5 percent, assuming that there are no ties for monthly lows. Then you can take the numbers 3, 5, and 5 percent to an online binomial distribution calculator to get a probability of this happening by chance of 0.1 percent, or one in a thousand. Try it on your own!

7 Assuming a zero average return for the 99 percent non-backdated grants, the average pre-grant return for the whole sample would then be 1 percent × –400 percent + 99 percent × 0 percent = –4 percent.

References

Abrantes-Metz, R., M. Kraten, A. Metz, and G. Seow. "LIBOR Manipulation?" *Journal of Banking and Finance* 36, no. 1 (2012): 136–150.

Apple Newsroom, "Apple Board of Directors Announces CEO Compensation," press release, January 19, 2000, https://www.apple.com/newsroom/2000/01/19Apple-Board-of-Directors-Announces-CEO-Compensation/.

Arvedlund, Erin. *Open Secret: The Global Banking Conspiracy That Swindled Investors Out of Billions*. New York: Portfolio, 2014.

Arvedlund, Erin. *Too Good to Be True: The Rise and Fall of Bernie Madoff*. New York: Portfolio, 2009.

Bandler, James, and Charles Forelle. "How a Giant Insurer Decided to Oust Hugely Successful CEO." *Wall Street Journal*, December 7, 2006.

Bollen, Nicolas P. B., and Veronika K. Pool. "Do Hedge Fund Managers Misreport Returns? Evidence from the Pooled Distribution." *Journal of Finance* 64, no. 5 (2009): 2257–2288.

Bollen, Nicolas P. B., and Veronika K. Pool. "Suspicious Patterns in Hedge Fund Returns and the Risk of Fraud." *Review of Financial Studies* 25, no. 9 (2012): 2673–2702.

Burgstahler, David, and Ilia Dichev. "Earnings Management to Avoid Earnings Decreases and Losses." *Journal of Accounting and Economics* 24, no. 1 (1997): 99–126.

Carreyrou, John. *Bad Blood: Secrets and Lies in a Silicon Valley Startup*. New York: Knopf, 2018.

Christie, William G., Jeffrey H. Harris, and Paul H. Schultz. "Why Did NASDAQ Market Makers Stop Avoiding Odd-Eighth Quotes?" *Journal of Finance* 49, no. 5 (1994): 1841–1860.

Christie, William G., and Paul H. Schultz. "Why Did NASDAQ Market Makers Avoid Odd-Eighth Quotes?" *Journal of Finance* 49, no. 5 (1994): 1813–1840.

Cicero, David C. "The Manipulation of Executive Stock Option Exercise Strategies: Information Timing and Backdating." *Journal of Finance* 64, no. 6 (2009): 2627–2663.

Cohen, Daniel A., and Paul Zarowin. "Accrual-based and Real Earnings Management Activities around Seasoned Equity Offerings." *Journal of Accounting and Economics* 50, no. 1 (2010): 2–19.

Cohen, Lauren, Christopher Malloy, and Lukasz Pomorski. "Decoding Inside Information." *Journal of Finance* 67, no. 3 (2012): 1009–1043.

Eichenwald, Kurt. *A Conspiracy of Fools: A True Story*. New York: Broadway Books, 2005.

Elkind, Peter. *Rough Justice: The Rise and Fall of Eliot Spitzer*. New York: Portfolio, 2010.

Enrich, David. *The Spider Network: How a Math Genius and a Gang of Scheming Bankers Pulled Off One of the Greatest Scams in History*. New York: HarperCollins, 2017.

Fandos, Nicholas, and Katie Benner. "Justice Dept. Ends Stock Trade Inquiry into Richard Burr without Charges." *New York Times*, January 19, 2021.

Fang, Vivian W., Allen H. Huang, and Jonathan M. Karpoff. "Short Selling and Earnings Management: A Controlled Experiment." *Journal of Finance* 71, no. 3 (2016): 1251–1294.

Forelle, Charles, and James Bandler. "The Perfect Payday." *Wall Street Journal*, March 18, 2006.

Gregoriou, Greg N., and Francois-Serge Lhabitant. "Madoff: A Flock of Red Flags." *Journal of Wealth Management* 12, no. 1 (2009): 89–97.

Griffin, John M., Samuel Kruger, and Prateek Mahajan. "Did FinTech Lenders Facilitate PPP Fraud?" *Journal of Finance* 78, no. 3 (2023): 1777–1827.

Griffin, John M., and Gonzalo Maturana. "Who Facilitated Misreporting in Securitized Loans?" *Review of Financial Studies* 29, no. 2 (2016): 384–419.

Guth, Robert A., and Justin Scheck. "The Man Who Wired Silicon Valley." *Wall Street Journal*, December 28, 2009.

Hays, Constance L. "Martha Stewart Indicted by U.S. On Obstruction." *New York Times*, June 5, 2003.

Hays, Constance L., and Patrick McGeehan. "A Closer Look at Martha Stewart's Trades." *New York Times*, July 15, 2002.

REFERENCES

Henriques, Diana B. *The Wizard of Lies: Bernie Madoff and the Death of Trust.* New York: Times Books, 2011.

Houge, Todd, and Jay Wellman. "Fallout from the Mutual Fund Trading Scandal." *Journal of Business Ethics* 62, no. 2 (2005): 129–139.

Jagolinzer, Alan D., David F. Larcker, Gaizka Ormazabal, and Daniel J. Taylor. "Political Connections and the Informativeness of Insider Trades." *Journal of Finance* 75, no. 4 (2020): 1833–1876.

Keefe, Patrick Radden. "The Empire of Edge." *New Yorker*, October 13, 2014.

Kolhatkar, Sheelah. *Black Edge: Inside Information, Dirty Money, and the Quest to Bring Down the Most Wanted Man on Wall Street.* New York: Random House, 2017.

Kovács, Balázs, David W. Lehman, and Glenn R. Carroll. "Grade Inflation in Restaurant Hygiene Inspections: Repeated Interactions between Inspectors and Restaurateurs." *Food Policy* 97 (2020): 1–10.

Lacetera, Nicola, Devin G. Pope, and Justin R. Sydnor. "Heuristic Thinking and Limited Attention in the Car Market." *American Economic Review* 102, no. 5 (2012): 2206–2236.

Lie, Erik. "On the Timing of CEO Stock Option Awards." *Management Science* 51, no. 5 (2005): 802–812.

Lie, Erik, and Randall A. Heron. "Does Backdating Explain the Stock Price Pattern around Executive Stock Option Grants?" *Journal of Financial Economics* 83, no. 2 (2007): 271–295.

Lie, Erik, and Randall A. Heron. "What Fraction of Stock Option Grants to Top Executives Have Been Backdated or Manipulated?" *Management Science* 55, no. 4 (2009): 513–525.

Ljungqvist, Alexander, Christopher Malloy, and Felicia Marston. "Rewriting History." *Journal of Finance* 64, no. 4 (2009): 1935–1960.

Malenko, Nadya, Joseph A. Grundfest, and Yao Shen. "Quadrophobia: Strategic Rounding of EPS Data." *Journal of Financial and Quantitative Analysis* 58, no. 8 (2023): 3231–3273.

Maremont, Mark. "Authorities Probe Improper Backdating of Options—Practice Allows Executives to Bolster Their Stock Gains: A Highly Beneficial Pattern." *Wall Street Journal*, November 11, 2005.

Masters, Brooke. *Spoiling for a Fight: The Rise of Eliot Spitzer.* New York: Times Books, 2006.

McCrum, Dan. "Wirecard and Me: Dan McCrum on Exposing a Criminal Enterprise." *Financial Times*, September 2, 2020.

McCrum, Dan, and Stefania Palma. "Wirecard Executive Suspected over Contracts." *Financial Times*, January 31, 2019.

McLean, Bethany, and Peter Elkind. *The Smartest Guys in the Room: The Amazing Rise and Scandalous Fall of Enron*. New York: Portfolio, 2003.

Mollenkamp, Carrick. "Libor Fog: Bankers Cast Doubt on Key Rate amid Crisis." *Wall Street Journal*, April 16, 2008.

Mollenkamp, Carrick, and Mark Whitehouse. "Study Casts Doubt on Key Rate—WSJ Analysis Suggests Banks May Have Reported Flawed Interest Data for Libor." *Wall Street Journal*, May 30, 2008.

Norris, Floyd. "A Crime So Large It Changed the Law." *New York Times*, July 14, 2005.

Packer, George. "A Dirty Business." *New Yorker*, June 27, 2011.

Pulliam, Susan. "Fund Chief Snared by Taps, Turncoats." *Wall Street Journal*, December 29, 2009.

Raghavan, Anita. *The Billionaire's Apprentice: The Rise of the Indian-American Elite and the Fall of the Galleon Hedge Fund*. New York: Business Plus, 2013.

Revell, Janice, and David Stires. "Making Sense of the Mutual Fund Scandal." *FORTUNE Magazine*, November 24, 2003.

Ritter, Jay R. "Forensic Finance." *Journal of Economics Perspectives* 22, no. 3 (2008): 127–147.

Schilit, Howard, and Jeremy Perler. *Financial Shenanigans: How to Detect Accounting Gimmicks and Fraud in Financial Reports*. New York: McGraw-Hill, 2018.

Stecklow, Steve. "Stock-Options Scandal Fugitive Puts Roots Down in Namibia." *Wall Street Journal*, November 17, 2006.

Urry, Maggie. "NASDAQ Uses Fresh Studies to Reject Collusion Claims." *Financial Times*, April 6, 1995.

Warren, Ben, and Julie Wernau. "Legal Marijuana Contains Dangerous Mold—States Approve It Anyway." *Wall Street Journal*, October 17, 2024.

Wells, Rob. "Lawsuits, New Study Allege Collusion in Nasdaq Market." *Associated Press*, July 26, 1994.

Wells, Rob. "Nasdaq Rolls Out Academic Heavies to Rebut Collusion Allegations." *Associated Press*, April 5, 1995.

West, Phil. "Nobel Laureate Chides Former Students over Nasdaq Papers." *Associated Press*, April 6, 1995.

Yang, Jing. "Behind the Fall of China's Luckin Coffee: A Network of Fake Buyers and a Fictitious Employee." *Wall Street Journal*, May 28, 2020.

Yermack, David. "Deductio' ad Absurdum: CEOs Donating Their Own Stock to Their Own Family Foundations." *Journal of Financial Economics* 94, no. 1 (2009): 107–123.

Yermack, David. "Good Timing: CEO Stock Option Awards and Company News Announcements." *Journal of Finance* 52, no. 2 (1997): 449–476.

Zitzewitz, Eric. "How Widespread Was Late Trading in Mutual Funds?" *American Economic Review* 96, no. 2 (2006): 284–289.

Zweig, Jason. "Ironing Out an Investing Mystery." *Wall Street Journal*, November 9, 2019.

Acknowledgments

I am indebted to Melanie Alexander and Randy Heron for their assistance in developing the material and editing this book, and to my editor, Jeevan Sivasubramaniam, for promoting the project and providing guidance. Many other individuals, including Kelli Christiansen, Rob Ellman, Michelle Lam, Kathy Scheiern, and past students, have also provided helpful feedback.

Index

Numbers
2-and-20 compensation, 43, 44, 46
60 Minutes, 97, 98

A
abnormal stock returns, 128–130, 140
Access International, 47
accountants/accounting
    how to detect manipulation, 72–75
    MTM accounting, 63–65, 66–68, 75
    statement manipulation, 58, 62
accruals management, 75, 78, 79
Agius, Marcus, 119
Akamai, 94
Alexander, Kobi, 137–139
Alipay, 70
Alliance Capital, 34
alpha returns, 43, 83
altruism, 55
American Economic Review, 35
AMEX stocks, 16
anticompetitive practices, 20
AOL, 63
Apple, 15, 16, 18–19
Arthur Andersen, 66–69
Arvedlund, Erin, 49
Ashford, Evelyn, 2
ask-bid spreads, 13, 17, 45
at-the-money option grants, 123, 124, 127
auditing/auditors
    and conflicts of interest, 59
    regulatory reforms for, 71–72
    uncovering fraud via, 75
    of Wirecard, 73

B
Bacanovic, Peter, 85–87
Bachus, Spencer, 97, 102
backdated option grants, x, 39, 121–122, 125,
    126–128, 129–141
*Bad Blood: Secrets and Lies in a Silicon
    Valley Startup* (Carreyrou), 72
balance sheets, 59, 67
Banco Santander, 46
Bank of America, 32
Bank of England, 112
Bank of Japan, 116, 117
bankruptcies, 65–66, 69
bank stability, 110–111
bapineuzumab, 89–90
Barclays, 112, 119
Barron's, 49, 50
Bear Stearns, 20
behavioral economics, 74
benchmarking, 1–5, 6, 34, 109
benchmarks
    accruals and, 78
    and analyst incentives, 4
    and earnings management, 73–74
    identifying fraud via, 2
    LIBOR rate, 105, 111, 114, 120
    for mutual fund inflow/performance, 34
    normal stock returns as, 101, 128
    and salami slicing, 16
    S&P 500 as, 43, 47
Bernanke, Ben, 97
bid-ask spreads, 13, 17, 45
bill-and-hold sales, 62–63
Bingaman, Anne, 21

black edge, 83
Blockbuster Video, 67–68
Boehner, John, 97
Bogle, Jack, 28
Bollen, Nick, 52, 53
bonds, 114, 139–140
borrowing rates, 110–111, 112
Brandeis, Louis D., 145
Braun, Markus, xi, 72, 73
Briloff, Abraham, 57
Bristol Myers, 84
Brocade Communications Systems, 135
Brown, David, 27, 31
Bruno, Joe, 37
Buffett, Warren, 43, 93, 95
Burgstahler, David, 76
Burr, Richard, 99
Bush, George W., 121
Bush family, 66
BusinessWeek, 121

C

call options, 47, 123
Canary Capital Management, 30, 31, 32–33
Carreyrou, John, 72–73
Carroll, Glenn, 6
Casey, Frank, 47, 48, 49
cash flow, earnings vs., 75, 78
CDSs (credit default swaps), 114
Chais, Stanley, 46
charitable gifts, 141, 143
Chiesi, Danielle, 94
Chinese firms
    earnings auditing for, 76–77
    Luckin Coffee, 69–71
    U.S. relations with, 71, 72
Christie, Bill, 15–20, 23
Cicero, David, 141
Cigna, 96
Citigroup, 107, 112, 114, 119
class action suits
    and backdated options, 132, 134
    blowback from, 23
    and estimated EPS, 77–78
    against Luckin Coffee, 71
    NASDAQ collusion case, 20, 22, 23
Cohen, Daniel, 79
Cohen, Lauren, 100
Cohen, Steve, 81, 89–91
collar investment strategy, 47, 50
Comey, James, 85, 86

Comverse Technology, 135–139
conflicts of interest
    and accurate LIBOR rate, 107, 120
    analyst/banker ties and, 27
    for financial statement auditors, 59
    within hedge funds, 44, 45
    for John Boehner, 97
    for stock analysts, 4
congress members, insider trading by, 97–99
Continenza, Jim, 142–143
corporate executives. *See* executives
corporations
    backdated option grants at, 121–122, 134,
        140–141
    bill-and-hold sales by, 62–63
    earnings auditing for, 76–78
    earnings of, 60–65, 73
    effects of fraud at, 145
    Enron, 66–69
    forensic economics and fraudulent, x
    glorifying statements at, 59, 60–61, 74,
        75–79
    insider trading at, 82, 95–96
    Luckin Coffee, 69–71
    maximizing stock price of, 60–61, 63–64
    option grants and expenses of, 124
    price fixing by, 5
    regulatory reforms for, 71–72
    SPV subsidiaries of, 65
covenant violation, 73, 74
COVID-19 pandemic, 99, 142, 146
Cox, Chris, 51, 135
credit default swaps (CDSs), 114
credit risk, 108
credit spread, 108, 113, 114
credit terms, lenient, 79
Cuban, Mark, 41
Cuomo, Andrew, 37

D

Darin, Roger, 117
data patterns
    to detect earnings management, 75–79
    distribution disruptions, 5–9
    exposing fraud via, x, 145
    in hedge fund returns, 52–53
    for insider trading, 100
    lack of data points, 3
    public access to, 9–10
    systematic concealment of, 4–5
    and trading in eighths, 15–16

dating app fraud, 5
day trading, 13, 23, 29, 142
debt burdens, 65, 66, 67, 110–111
debt restructuring, 68
decimalization, 14
Defense Production Act, 142
de la Villahuchet, Rene-Thierry Magon, 47
Department of Justice, 91, 99
derivatives, 44, 105, 111, 117
Deutsche Bank, 107, 120
Diamond, Bob, 119
Dichev, Ilia, 76
Dieselgate, 3–4
discretionary accruals, 78, 79
distribution disruptions, 1, 5–9
drug testing, 2

E

earnings management, 60–65, 66, 73,
    75–79, 124
earnings per share (EPS), 60, 61, 64, 77
edge, investment, 43, 83
Elan, 89, 90, 100
emissions scandal, Volkswagen, 3–4
Emperors Club, 37–38
energy industry, 66
Enrich, David, 116
Enron, 58, 65–69, 75, 132
equity sales, 74, 79
Erbitux, 84, 85, 87
Everson, Mark, 135
exchange traded funds (ETFs), 97
executives
    account glorification by, 62–66
    boasting by, 72
    call options and performance of, 123
    compensation for, 122–124, 133
    earnings targets for, 74, 75–76
    effects of fraud by, 79, 145
    financial incentives for, 57–58
    income tax for, 123, 143–144
    insider information of, 125–126, 128
    insider trading by, 95–96, 99–100
    LIBOR manipulation by bank, 116, 119
    option grants for, ix–x, 121–124, 126–127,
        135–139, 140–141
    and political intelligence, 101–103
    regulatory reforms for, 71–72
    tax evasion by, 141, 143–144
exercise price, 123, 124
EY auditing firm, 73

F

Fairfield Greenwich Group, 45, 50
Fairfield Sentry Limited Fund, 45, 47, 48
fair value accounting, 63–65
False Claims Act, 147
Farr, Terry, 117, 118
Fastow, Andy, 66–69
Federal Open Market Committee (FOMC),
    106–107
Federal Reserve System, 106–107, 112
Fed funds rate, 106
financial sector
    2008 crisis in, 7, 51, 93, 97, 101, 102, 108
    analyst bias in, 4
    data availability for, 10
    Eliot Spitzer vs., 26
    forensic economics for, x
    importance of LIBOR to, 111
    lack of altruism in, 55
    LIBOR rigging and, 105
    open fraud in, 120
    trading costs, 12–13
financial statements
    glorification of, 57–58, 62–66
    organizational purpose of, 59
    SPVs and modification of, 65
Financial Times, 73
Fiorina, Carly, 1
First Step Act, 95
Food and Drug Administration (FDA), 84,
    85, 87
forensic economics, x–xi, 145, 147
forward pricing rule, 28, 29, 36
fraud, systemic
    accruals management, 78
    backdated option grants, x, 39, 121–122,
        125–141
    by Bernie Madoff, 45–52
    corporate price fixing, 5–6
    earning manipulation, 73–74
    Eliot Spitzer vs., 26
    at Enron, 65–69
    executive tax evasion, 141
    in the financial sector, x
    forensic economics for, x, 147
    in hedge fund industry, 41, 44–45,
        52–55
    hiding in plain sight, 120
    increased scrutiny vs., 145
    invitation to uncover, xi
    LIBOR manipulation, 105, 108, 112–115

fraud, systemic (*continued*)
    at Luckin Coffee, 69–71
    mutual fund late trading, 30–34
    at NASDAQ, 15–17, 20–22
    on PPP applications, 146–147
    and real-estate refinancing, 8–9
    regulatory reforms to address, 71–72
    and risk/return dynamic, 47, 48, 52
    salami slicing, 11
    at start-ups, 72
    against stock investors, 13
    at Theranos, 72–73
    and trading in eighths, 15–19
    on Wall Street, 25–26
    widespread effects of, 145
    at Wirecard, 73
    See also insider trading
Freedom of Information Act (FOIA), 10
funds of funds, investing in, 44

G

Galleon Group, 92–95
Garcia, Michael, 38
Gekko, Gordon, 81
generally accepted accounting principles
    (GAAP), 59, 72
Gerson Lehrman Group (GLG), 83, 88, 89
Gilman, Dr. Sid, 88, 100
Gilmour, Jim, 118
Gold, Nelson, 18
Goldman Sachs, 20, 22, 93, 94, 95
Goodman, Colin, 117, 118
Goodwin, Andrew, 31
Great Electrical Equipment Conspiracy, 5
Gregg, Judd, 98
Griffin, John, 8, 146
Grossman, Sanford, 20–21
Grundfest, Joseph, 76
Guardian, 39
Gupta, Rajat, 93, 95

H

Halifax Bank of Scotland (HBOS), 107, 110, 114
Hardiman, Joseph, 18
Harrington, Noreen, 30, 31
Harris, Jeff, 18, 19
Hastert, Dennis, 98
Hayes, Tom, 116–119
hedge funds
    avoiding fraudulent, 54
    of Bernie Madoff, 45–51

Galleon Group, 92, 93
    information sales to, 98
    insider trading by, 89–91
    investor profile, 43–44
    late trading and, 31
    management fees for, 42–43
    manager incentives, 43, 44
    misreporting on, 52–53
    vs. mutual funds, 42
    mutual funds as feeding, 44
    patterns of fraud in, 52–55
    performance deception by, 41
    risk-taking by, 43, 44
    Voyager Capital, 93
Heron, Randy, 131, 132, 133, 140
Holding Foreign Companies Accountable
    Act, 72
Holmes, Elizabeth, xi, 72–73
Houtkin, Harvey, 23

I

ICAP, 117–118
illegal insider trading, 82
ImClone, 81, 84–88
income statements, 59
income tax evasion, 141, 143–144
index funds, 43
Indiana University, 131
information, access to, 10
insider information
    executives' access to, 95–96, 99–100
    to generate alpha, 43
    and Madoff's scheme, 52
    for option grants, 125–126, 128
    political, 97, 101–103
    trading via, 82
insider trading
    difficulty of tracking, 99–100
    by executives, 95–96
    of ImClone, 84–88
    information access for, 81, 82–83
    at Kodak, 142–143
    by members of congress, 97–99
    and political intelligence, 97–99,
        101–103
    by politicians, 97–99, 101–103
    prevalence of, 100–101
    by Raj Rajaratnam, 92–95
    role of GLG in, 83–84
    by SAC Capital, 88–91
Intel, 93

interest rates
    Fed funds rate, 106–107
    LIBOR rate, 108, 109, 111
    SOFR and, 120
    Treasury yield, 106, 108, 109
Internal Revenue Service, 135
investment, stock
    based on inside information, 82, 83
    Bernie Madoff as advisor for, 45–46
    buy-and-hold for, 13
    and corporate stock pricing, 60–61
    in funds of funds, 44
    in hedge funds, 43–44
    in individual stock vs. portfolios, 34
    in Kodak, 142
    late-trading privileges for, 32
    long- vs. short-term, 29, 79
    in Luckin Coffee, 70
    mutual fund fees, 27–28, 33
investment bankers, 27
IPOs, 27, 70, 98
"Is LIBOR Broken?" (Peng), 112

J

Jarrell, Professor Gregg, 95
Jobs, Steve, ix, 72, 122
Journal of Finance, 17, 19, 20, 23, 100, 101, 132
Journal of Financial Economics, 132
*Journal of the American Medical
    Association*, 83
Joyner, Florence Griffith (Flo-Jo), 1–2
justice initiatives, xi

K

Karfunkel, George, 143
Ketchum, Richard, 18
Khan, Roomy, 93
Kodak, 142–144
Kovács, Balázs, 6
KPMG, 73
Kroft, Seve, 97
Kruger, Samuel, 146
Kumar, Anil, 93, 95

L

late trading
    by Canary Capital Management, 32–33
    covering of tracks for, 33
    defined, 25
    market evidence of, 34–36
    of mutual funds, 29–31, 32–34

LA Times, 18
Lay, Ken, 58, 66–69
Lehman, David, 6
Lehman Brothers, 93, 109
Levy, Norman, 46
Lewis, Michael, 25
Lexecon, 21
"Libor Fog: Bankers Cast Doubt on Key Rate
    Amid Crisis" (Mollenkamp), 112
LIBOR rate
    calculating the, 106–108
    fines for the manipulation of, 119–120
    as industry benchmark, 105
    manipulation of, 108–109, 112–115
    panel bank submissions and, 107–108,
        110–111, 112–113, 115, 117–119
    players in manipulation scheme, 115–119
    replacement of, 120
    unintentional adjustments to, 110
liquidity, stock, 13, 14, 18
"Liquidity and Market Structure" (Grossman
    and Miller), 20
Ljungqvist, Alexander, 4
loan covenant violation, 73, 74
loan-to-value (LTV) ratio, 7–9
London Stock Exchange, 29
Los Angeles Times, 17
Luckin Coffee, 65, 69–71, 72

M

Madoff, Bernie, 41–42, 45–52
Mahajan, Prateek, 146
Malenko, Nadya, 76
Malloy, Christopher, 4, 100
Maremont, Mark, 134
MARHedge, 49
marijuana industry fraud, 7–8
market timing, 29, 31
Markopolos, Harry, 48–49, 50
mark-to-market (MTM) accounting, 63–65,
    66–68, 75
Marston, Felicia, 4
Martha Stewart Living Omnimedia, 87
Martoma, Mathew, 89–91, 100
Maturana, Gonzalo, 8
McGuire, Bill, 139
McKinsey, 66, 93
Mercury Interactive Corp., 133
Merrill Lynch, 20, 22, 85
Milberg Weiss, 20
Milken, Michael, 96

Miller, Merton, 20–21
mispricings, stock, 46
Modigliani, Franco, 20
Modigliani-Miller theorem, 20
Mollenkamp, Carrick, 112–115
Morgan Stanley, 22
mutual funds
    defined, 27
    duping of long-term investors in, 32, 36
    evidence of fraudulent trading on, 34–36
    fees for, 27, 33–34, 36
    forward pricing rule for, 28
    vs. hedge funds, 42
    hedge funds as fed by, 44
    late trading of, 29–36
    long- vs. short-term investment in, 29,
        31, 32
    past vs. future performance of, 34
    privileged trading on, 32
    returns/inflow correlation for, 34
    valuation of, 28–29

N

NASDAQ, 14, 15–20, 70, 71
National Association of Realtors (NAR), 6
National Association of Securities Dealers
    (NASD), 18, 21, 22, 23
Needham & Co, 92
negative return adjustment, 52–53
Nesfield, James, 31
Nesfield Capital, 31
net asset value (NAV), 28, 29–30, 35
Netflix, 88
New York Mets, 81, 91
New York Stock Exchange (NYSE)
    decimalization of, 14
    NASDAQ trading vs., 16
    SOX Act and, 71
    trading hours for, 25, 28–29
New York Times, 38, 88
New York University, 128
nondiscretionary accruals, 78
non-recurring earnings, 61

O

Obama, Barak, 98
Ocrant, Michael, 49
off-balance sheet financing, 65
Olson, Mark, 135
Olympic world records, 1–2
Ontrak, 96

opportunistic trades, 100
option grants
    author's investigation of, 128–130
    backdated, ix–x, 121–122, 125, 126–127,
        129–140
    case studies of backdated, 135–140
    Comverse and UnitedHealth fraud, 135–139
    as executive compensation, 122–124
    and insider information, 125–126
    legality of backdated, 127–128
    market evidence of, 128–130, 131
    prevalence of backdated, 140–141
    process of issuing, 124–125
    WSJ research into, 133–134

P

Paulson, Hank, 97
Paycheck Protection Program (PPP),
    146–147
PCAOB (Public Company Accounting
    Oversight Board), 71, 72, 135
Peizer, Terren, 96
Pelosi, Nancy, 98
Peng, Scott, 112
penny shaving schemes, 11
P/E ratio (price-to-earnings), 60, 61, 64
"Perfect Payday, The" (*WSJ*), 134
performance-enhancing drugs, 2
Petty, Richard, ix
Picower, Jeffry, 46
Point72 Asset Management, 91
politics
    fall of Eliot Spitzer, 36–39
    political intelligence industry, 97–99,
        101–103
Pomorski, Lukasz, 100
Ponzi, Charles, 54
Ponzi schemes, 45–52, 54
Pool, Veronika, 52, 53
portfolios
    managers of, 27
    risk/return balance in, 47
    securities, 27, 28–29, 54
Prairie Parkway, 98
price clustering, 21
price discounts, 79
price fixing, 5
price-to-earnings (P/E) ratio, 60, 61, 64
prosecutorial misconduct, 37–38
Protégé Partners LLC, 43
proxy statements, 125, 131

Public Company Accounting Oversight
Board (PCAOB), 71, 72, 135
Pulitzer Prize for Public Service, x, 134
put options, 47

R
Rabobank, 118, 120
Rajaratnam, Raj, 81, 91–95
Ravazzolo, Fabiola, 112
Read, Darrell, 117, 118
real earnings management, 79
real estate market
    pre-2008 refinancing transactions, 7–9
    price clustering in, 21
    realtor collusion in, 5
recurring earnings, 61
reference points, 74
refinancing practices, pre-2008, 8
regulatory reforms, 71–72
repurchase agreements (repos), 120
researchers
    data access for, 10
    forensic economics for, xi
    journalistic excellence, 114–115
restaurant hygiene scores, 6–7
retirement accounts, 79
returns on assets, 76, 100
risk-free interest rate, 108
risk/return dynamic, 47, 48, 52–53, 54
Robinhood Markets, Inc., 12, 13, 142
Robson, Paul "Pooks," 118
routine trades, 100
Royal Bank of Canada (RBC), 117
Royal Bank of Scotland, 116, 120
Russell 2000, 13

S
SAC Capital Advisors, 89–91, 100
salami slicing, 11
Sánchez-Vizcaíno Mengual, Eloy, xi
S and P 100, 47
S and P 500, 13, 43, 47, 53–54, 102, 122
Sarbanes, Paul, 71
Sarbanes-Oxley (SOX) Act, 71–72
scheduled grants, 128
Schultz, George, 72
Schultz, Paul, 15–20, 23
Secured Overnight Financing Rate (SOFR), 120
Securities and Exchange Commission (SEC)
    as data source, 10
    and decimalization, 14
    Enron investigation, 67, 68, 69
    executives as regulated by, 99–100
    Galleon investigation, 93, 94–95
    hedge fund regulation by, 44–45
    ImClone investigation, 86, 87
    late trading investigation, 50
    Madoff investigation, 48–51
    and NASDAQ price fixing, 20
    option grant filing with, 125, 126, 130, 131, 134
    option grant investigation, x, 130, 132, 133
    persecution of false advertising, 41
    SOX Act and, 71
securities portfolios
    calculating pricing for, 28–29
    of hedge funds, 54
    laws governing, 82
    mutual funds as comprised of, 27
Security Trust Company (STC), 32–33
Shapiro, Carl, 46
Shen, Yao, 76
short-term earnings, 62
Skandal! Bringing Down Wirecard, 73
Skilling, Jeff, 58, 66–69
Smith Breeden Prize, 23
SOES (Small-Order Execution System), 23
Spanish silver dollars, 14
special-purpose vehicles (SPVs), 65, 67, 75
The Spider Network (Enrich), 116
Spitzer, Eliot, 25–27, 30–32, 33, 36–39
split/strike investment strategy, 47, 50
spreads, bid-ask, 13, 17, 45
Stern, Eddie, 30, 32
Stern, Leonard, 30
Stevenson, Robert Louis, 11
Stewart, Martha, 81, 84–88
stock analysts
    bias of, 4
    conflicts of interest for, 27
    fraud detection by, 75
stock brokers, 12, 14, 29, 33, 45, 85, 87, 116–118
stock dealers/market makers, 11, 13–14, 15, 17, 18, 19, 20, 45, 49
stock market
    buy-and-hold strategy in, 13
    corporate stock prices, 60–61, 63–64, 67
    decimalization for, 14
    EPS manipulation and, 77
    hedge fund value alignment with, 53–54
    international trading hours, 28, 29, 35–36
    mispricings in, 46
    mutual fund trading on, 27–30

option grants and abnormal returns in, 128–130
price clustering in, 21
trader influence on LIBOR, 111
stock transactions
  by Bernie Madoff, 45
  bid-ask spreads in, 13, 18
  day trading, 13, 23, 29
  enhanced oversight of, 22
  evidence of late trading, 34–36
  insider info for. *see* insider trading
  salami slicing and, 11
  SOES trading, 23
  trading costs, 12–13
  trading in eighths and, 14, 15–16, 18
Stoll, Hans, 21
Stone, Roger, 37, 38
Stop Trading on Congressional Knowledge (STOCK) Act, 98–99
"Study Casts Doubt on Key Rate" (Mollenkamp and Whitehouse), 114
Sunbeam, 63

T

target rate, Federal Reserve, 106–107
tax evasion, 141, 143–144
Theranos, xi, 72–73
Thomson Reuters, 107
TIBOR (Tokyo Interbank Offered Rate), 117
Time, x, 39, 73
Tokyo Stock Exchange (TSE), 28, 30
trading costs, 12–13
Treasury yield, 106, 108, 109, 113
Troopergate, 37
Troubled Asset Relief Program (TARP), 102, 103
Trump, Donald, 72, 95, 142
Tucker, Jeffrey, 50
Twenty Acre Capital LP, 41

U

UBS, 117–119
Under Armour, 63
unethical practices
  accruals management, 78, 79
  backdated option grants. x, 39, 121–122, 125–141
  by Bernie Madoff, 45–52
  compromised stock analysts, 4
  corporate price fixing, 5–6
  earnings management, 60–65, 66, 73, 75–78

executive tax evasion, 141
  familiarity and, 6–7
  glorification of financial health, 57–58
  in hedge funds, 44–45
  increased scrutiny vs., 19, 145
  late trading, 29–30
  LIBOR manipulation, 108
  mutual fund market timing fraud, 30–34
  at NASDAQ, 15–17, 20–22
  on PPP applications, 146–147
  quid pro quo arrangements, 8
  regulatory reforms to address, 71–72
  salami slicing, 11
  trading in eighths, 15–19
  widespread effects of, 145
  See also insider trading
UnitedHealth Group, 135–139
University of Michigan, 88
unscheduled grants, 129
US International Development Finance Corporation (DFC), 142
US Justice Department, 20, 21, 22

V

Vanderbilt University, 23
Vanguard, 28
Volkswagen (VW) emissions scandal, 3–4
Voyager Capital, 95

W

Wall Street Journal, x, 7, 18, 73, 112, 113, 130, 133–134
Waskal, Harlan, 84–85
Waskal, Sam, 84–85, 87
Watkins, Sherron, 68
WeChat, 70
Wellick, Tyrell, 105
Westdeutsche Landesbank, 114
Whitehouse, Mark, 113–115
Wirecard, xi, 73
WorldCom, 65, 66, 69, 71, 132
WrestleMania, 12, 21
Wyeth, 89, 90, 100

Y

Yermack, David, 128, 141

Z

Zarowin, Paul, 79
zero earnings, 74
Zitzewitz, Eric, 34, 36

About the Author

ERIK LIE is a professor of finance and the head of the finance department at the University of Iowa. He grew up in Porsgrunn, Norway, as one of three kids of a children's librarian and a civil engineer. In 1988, he moved to the United States to attend the University of Oregon. After serving in the Norwegian Navy from 1991 to 1992, he completed his PhD at Purdue University in 1996.

Lie began his academic career at the College of William & Mary, where he spent eight years before moving to the University of Iowa. Both in his teaching and research, he has developed a fascination with human behavior and incentives. This has led him to intriguing discoveries, especially in the corporate world. In 2002, Lie began researching executive compensation. Using large databases, he documented strong patterns of manipulation of stock option grants, which he brought to the attention of the Securities and Exchange Commission (SEC) and the *Wall Street Journal* in 2005. This culminated in a massive SEC investigation, countless lawsuits, congressional hearings, the firing of at least seventy corporate executives, and the *Wall Street Journal*'s only Pulitzer Prize for Public Service to date. His contribution was also recognized outside the academic world when *Time* magazine included him on its list of the one hundred most influential people in the world.

Lie lives in Iowa City, the first United States UNESCO City of Literature and the location of the Iowa Writer's Workshop. He enjoys spending time with his family and staying engaged in various sports, ranging from the ordinary, like running and soccer, to the more obscure, like squash, skiing, and windsurfing.

Berrett–Koehler
Publishers

Berrett-Koehler is an independent publisher dedicated to an ambitious mission: *Connecting people and ideas to create a world that works for all.*

Our publications span many formats, including print, digital, audio, and video. We also offer online resources, training, and gatherings. And we will continue expanding our products and services to advance our mission.

We believe that the solutions to the world's problems will come from all of us, working at all levels: in our society, in our organizations, and in our own lives. Our publications and resources offer pathways to creating a more just, equitable, and sustainable society. They help people make their organizations more humane, democratic, diverse, and effective (and we don't think there's any contradiction there). And they guide people in creating positive change in their own lives and aligning their personal practices with their aspirations for a better world.

And we strive to practice what we preach through what we call "The BK Way." At the core of this approach is *stewardship,* a deep sense of responsibility to administer the company for the benefit of all of our stakeholder groups, including authors, customers, employees, investors, service providers, sales partners, and the communities and environment around us. Everything we do is built around stewardship and our other core values of *quality, partnership, inclusion,* and *sustainability.*

We are grateful to our readers, authors, and other friends who are supporting our mission. We ask you to share with us examples of how BK publications and resources are making a difference in your lives, organizations, and communities at bkconnection.com/impact.

Dear reader,

Thank you for picking up this book and welcome to the worldwide BK community! You're joining a special group of people who have come together to create positive change in their lives, organizations, and communities.

What's BK all about?

Our mission is to connect people and ideas to create a world that works for all.

Why? Our communities, organizations, and lives get bogged down by old paradigms of self-interest, exclusion, hierarchy, and privilege. But we believe that can change. That's why we seek the leading experts on these challenges—and share their actionable ideas with you.

A welcome gift

To help you get started, we'd like to offer you a **free copy** of one of our bestselling ebooks:

bkconnection.com/welcome

When you claim your **free ebook**, you'll also be subscribed to our blog.

Our freshest insights

Access the best new tools and ideas for leaders at all levels on our blog at ideas.bkconnection.com.

Sincerely,

Your friends at Berrett-Koehler